STRATEGY
OF
SERVICE

SOS

. . . ——— . . .

STRATEGY
OF
SERVICE

JUNE A. WILLIAMS

Ministry
Resources
Library

Zondervan Publishing House • Grand Rapids, MI

Strategy of Service
Copyright © 1984 by the Zondervan Corporation
Grand Rapids, Michigan

Ministry Resources Library is an imprint of Zondervan Publishing House,
1415 Lake Drive, S.E., Grand Rapids, Michigan

Library of Congress Cataloging in Publication Data
Williams, June A.
    Strategy of service.
    1. Church charities—United States.   2. Church
charities—Study and teaching—United States.   I. Title.
HV530.W54   1984   361.7'5   84-19572
ISBN 0-310-45761-0

All Scripture quotations, unless otherwise noted, are taken from the
HOLY BIBLE: NEW INTERNATIONAL VERSION (North American
Edition), copyright © 1978 by the International Bible Society. Used by
permission of Zondervan Bible Publishers.

Edited by Michael G. Smith
Designed by Louise Bauer

Printed in the United States of America

84 85 86 87 88 89 / 10 9 8 7 6 5 4 3 2 1

To the memory of
The Rev. Herman A. Spinney,
who said I would write a book someday.

Contents

	Foreword	**9**
	Preface	**11**
1.	Call Out the Reserves!	**13**
2.	Journey Into Service	**15**
3.	The Paradox	**21**
4.	Looking Back, Looking Ahead	**25**
5.	Journey Out of Bitterness	**27**
6.	Seminary—the Long and the Short of It	**34**
7.	Growing Pains	**41**
8.	Clustering Churches to Network a Neighborhood	**45**
9.	Clues for Clergy	**57**
10.	People Need People	**64**
11.	The Ministry of Listening	**72**
12.	Setting Up a Plan of Action	**79**
13.	Clues for Continuing	**86**
14.	Another Possibility	**96**
	Postscript: Once Again, Lightly	**101**
	Appendix 1 Commitment Form	**105**
	Appendix 2 File Cards	**107**
	Appendix 3 Volunteer Service Record	**109**
	Appendix 4 Certificate of Achievement	**110**

Foreword

It was at the monthly meeting of Baptist ministers that I was first introduced to Willie Williams and her unique ministry. She very articulately presented the concept of ministering to people in need, which she called "Strategy of Service." The program was unique in that the strategy called for trained volunteers, trained as thoroughly as any Sunday school teacher would be, and a simple lay-led organization.

The church I served had a mission-action committee that was set up to minister to church families in crisis situations. They were armed only with their spirit of willingness to serve! How much better if they could be equipped not only with that willing spirit, a very necessary ingredient for service, but also with skill and confidence. They then would be able to serve not only church members, but also people in the larger community.

So a schedule was set up for Willie to come and conduct a Strategy of Service seminar on four consecutive Sunday evenings. Publicity was given through the church bulletin and newsletter. We anticipated that twenty-five people would attend, but were overwhelmed when fifty were present! Though only twenty-one received certificates for completing eight hours of training, forty volunteers were enlisted.

SOS is now a definite and permanent program of the church. Many people within the congregation and in the community have been ministered to. When phone calls come or people walk into the church office requesting assistance, it is good to know that the church staff can call on an SOS member to help meet the need. If there is an immediate need for food or clothes, it is good to know that

SOS members have filled the pantry and we need only to walk to it to supply the needy person.

I am grateful to the Lord for leading Willie our way and for her ministry in equipping our people for effective service. It is a valuable ministry because it is a lasting ministry.

Mori Hiratani
Pastor
First Baptist Church
Pearl City, Hawaii

Preface

My career in human services amounted to a double confrontation. I had to face the many unmet needs of people living in close proximity to neighborhood churches, yet I was forced to acknowledge the reluctance of most Christians to become personally involved in local ministries.

Why is there such a gulf between profession of faith and performance? Is the breakdown between what is said and what is done a matter of blatant unconcern or of bewildered unpreparedness?

This book assumes that when we fail to assist those in need within our church neighborhood, it is often because we have not been given adequate training or provided with meaningful support systems. It offers a Strategy of Service whereby we can learn to recognize human distress signals, then to respond to the SOS calls of our own day and our own communities.

I would like to express my deep appreciation to Frances Forkish who gave so unstintingly of her time and talents in the preparation of the manuscript. Her encouragement and her thoughtful suggestions, as well as her typing ability, gave shining witness to her dedication to Christ and to the work of his kingdom.

One

Call Out the Reserves!

I suppose that every Christian at one time or another feels alone in the work of the Lord. Like Elijah of old we cry out, "And I, even I only, am left." Translated into the jargon of today it might read, "God, I'm doing all the work and nobody helps me!"

Sound familiar?

The Lord had to remind Elijah that there were seven thousand others willing to be called upon—God's reserves, ready and waiting. The Almighty wasn't worried. It was Elijah who had the problem.

- Maybe he was a loner.
- Maybe he thought no one else could do the job as well as he could.
- Maybe he kept so busy he forgot to ask God to help him figure out a more effective strategy of service.
- And chances are he completely overlooked the availability of the seven thousand. It didn't occur to him to send out an SOS.

He hadn't been a boy scout. Elijah never learned

the Morse Code with its international distress signal: SOS, ... _ _ _ ...

Three dots, three dashes, three dots. Originally the letters stood for "Save Our Ship!" Today they signal distress in many kinds of emergencies and crises. When someone transmits that signal it means there is trouble, that help is needed.

Of course, it is futile to send out a signal unless someone is prepared to receive it. People in distress can signal SOS all day and all night, but unless someone is tuned in to receive the message so that a rescue party can be dispatched, the call for help is in vain. We can't expect someone to save our ship, or anybody else's ship for that matter, without another kind of SOS—a Strategy Of Service.

. . .   _ _ _   . . .

Two

Journey Into Service

We are commanded in God's Word to live as Christ lived, to love as he loved. In the Scriptures love means responsible caring, giving oneself for another, sacrificing one's own time, energy, and possessions. We are to be involved as he was involved in our suffering world.

Yet a very candid Christian woman speaks for most of us when she confesses, "I know I'm supposed to be Christ's hands and feet in this neighborhood. I am forever feeling guilty because I am not. But how do I start? I don't know where to begin."

Does she speak for you, too? I know exactly how she feels. My own background is so similar to hers. From early childhood I was instructed in God's plan of salvation through his Son, Jesus Christ. I was urged to give my heart and life into his keeping. I was taught how to pray, how to study the Bible, how to witness to my faith in Christ, how to tithe. And I was exhorted to reach out to the sick, the lonely, the helpless. Certainly enough sermons were preached about it. Only one thing was lacking. I was not taught *how* to do this. Neither the minister nor the deacons—no, not even my Sunday school teachers—ever took me in hand and demonstrated practical ways to go about helping people in crisis in the community around me—especially people who were strangers and not a part of our church family. It was assumed that I was born with this knowledge, that Christians automatically are the kind of good neighbors that Jesus talked about. It never dawned on anyone that I needed to be equipped for this aspect of ministry as for all others.

I blush to remember the extent of my service outside the four walls of our church. It consisted of bravely singing hymns with the youth group out on the church lawn before the Sunday evening services each summer. Once I recited a poem in the local jail during a Christmas pageant. Of course, there was Visitation Sunday every year when, reluctantly, we knocked on all the doors in a given area around the church to invite people to worship the Lord with us. And occasionally, when the pastor conducted an evangelistic meeting on the common behind the city hall where the street people loitered, we young people were herded along to help with the singing. We were scared, we were self-conscious, we were devoutly glad when it was over. We were blind to the hunger and sickness around us, to the opportunities for personal, practical ministry.

Sensitivity to the suffering of others isn't something with which we are born. As I look back over my life, I realize that the development of my own sensitivity was extremely slow.

It would be correct to say that I am a WASP, a white, Anglo-Saxon Protestant. My father was an Episcopalian from New England, my mother a quiet Baptist from New Brunswick, Canada. We lived in an average, middle-class neighborhood. All the houses on our block were occupied by the same families for the entire twenty years we lived there. Like the other children in the community, I attended a nearby elementary school from kindergarten through the eighth grade, then went on to the local high school for four years. It was a safe, sane, secure existence. There were individual tragedies and setbacks—these were Depressions days—but somehow they were absorbed or buffered by the orderliness of our small society. Only World War II succeeded in stirring the depths of our serene little world. My brothers and all the rest of the boys in the neighborhood enlisted. Suddenly everything was different! As soon as I finished high school I went to work in a defense plant. At the age of eighteen I became known as Willie the Welder.

The loneliness inside a welder's helmet invites introspection. As I watched the incising flame of my torch sending showers of sparks from the resisting steel, I pretended that the steel didn't want to be melted. It didn't want to be changed. It wanted to stay the way it was. But if it stayed as it was, it would be quite useless. It never could be a strong link in a long chain destined to secure the landing barges of the U.S. Marines as they established beachheads on the other side of the world where my brother was fighting. Instead, it would lie alone out in the factory yard, covered with mud and rust.

To fulfill its destiny, the heart of that link had to be reduced to a molten pool. Into that pool the purest steel available was melted till the two were one weld. The slightest flaw or bubble or blemish in the weld could mean disaster. Given sufficient strain, it would break. The two metals had to be one. Before a chain was allowed to leave the plant, it was heated till it glowed red, then pounded, beaten and stretched past all likelihood of war-time tension. Every link had to pass inspection. Only then could the chain be sent to the men at the front.

There in the semi-darkness under my welder's helmet, the game I had been playing turned into the voice of God speaking to me. The melting heart of the link was my own. The pure steel flowing into that heart was none other than the life of the Son of glory. The chain itself was his body, the church.

This was not my conversion. I had known and believed since childhood that the Lord Jesus loved me, that he was my Savior. Instead, it was a time of new awareness, of commitment, of redirection. I was hearing his call to service. Slowly, almost imperceptibly, changes occurred. God took his time with me. He knew my timidity. When World War II ended, I enrolled in a Christian college for a few years, then entered a school of nursing.

At the completion of nurses' training the insulation of my childhood and adolescence finally was penetrated. My first exposure to a different world came at the beginning of my career as a professional nurse. Friends hoped to enlist me for service on the foreign mission field. They suggested that I work at the Chicago Maternity Center first. In those days any woman going to the foreign field needed to know how to birth a baby without depending upon the conveniences of a modern hospital. Center nurses accompanied doctors into the slums of Chicago, assisting them as they delivered babies, often under very primitive conditions.

I spent one day "out on the District" as an observer with a Center crew, after which I literally ran, not walked, to the nearest shiny clean hospital, and became employed there instead. It took a full year for me to muster the courage to take a second look at the world of the Maternity Center.

When confronted by human distress, my first impulse was to retreat with the assurance that there was an agency to take care of that! How many Christians have given me this same reply when I have asked them to help someone in need. We are an agency-oriented society. We depend on agencies to protect us from having to respond to serious needs.

I find that it is those people who have suffered the most who are the first to reach out to others in distress. We learn sensitivity through our own pain. I recall vividly an incident that occurred while I worked in a hospital. I was summoned to comfort the relatives of a patient who was dying. They were crying so loudly they could be heard by all the patients on that floor. I led them into a room where I could shut the door so that their grief would be less audible. Suddenly the door opened. One of the patients stepped in. I knew her at once. She had been hospitalized for depression and despondency resulting from a marital breakup. She was, perhaps, the saddest, most wounded person on the floor. Yet she was the one who got out of her bed and followed the sounds of grief down the hall till she found us. She said softly, "I heard the crying. Oh, is there anything I can do to help?" Out of her pain she could reach out to others in pain.

While I was employed at the Chicago Maternity Center I spent hours, even days, in the most abject of slum dwellings attending women in labor. Poverty, hunger, disease, stark hopelessness paraded before me. But somehow my mind partitioned it off. It was my "job" to be there. When it was time to go off duty I stepped back into what, to me, was the real world— my world—full of creature comforts and plenty. We prattled on about "delivering a healthy baby to a healthy mother" without much thought of what would become of that mother and that baby once we left the premises. That was someone else's "job."

I remember being in one desperately poor home a week before Easter. The two-year-old in the family was playing with a tiny, fluffy chicken someone had given him. Its soft, yellow feathers were no protection against a toddler's eager fingers. I protested to the mother that a baby chicken was not a fit plaything for a baby boy. She said I could take the chicken with me when I left. In my preoccupation with attending her through her labor and delivery I forgot about it. That evening at home, I remembered. My concern for the chicken was such that it sent me back to the rescue. But I was too late. The tiny thing was nearly lifeless. I took it away, tried to revive it, but it died. I cried over the death of that chicken. But I felt no particular grief over the mother and babies I had left in that slum.

God used a personal crisis to shock me into oneness with the company of those who suffer. Injured and ill, three thousand miles away from home and family, I learned firsthand what fear and pain are all about. Month after despairing month passed before I was well enough to return to work. I found then that my nursing had acquired a new dimension. Suddenly, in a way I had never experienced before, I was acutely responsive to the fear and pain of my patients. At some point in my own dark hour a light had been turned on within me that could shine into the dark corridors of other lives. If God allows suffering to come your way, you can count on him to use it redemptively sooner or later.

· · · — — — · · ·

Three

The Paradox

"No exertion, no strain—and no foreign mission field."

The doctor's decision after that long illness devastated me. My neatly planned life suddenly seemed devoid of all direction. Instead of active, physical involvement as a nurse, I was forced to choose among less strenuous occupations on the fringe of my profession or in related health and social service fields. Looking back now, I can see God's hand in the dark decade that followed, but I could not see it then. All I knew then was that I hurt, that life was a grim affair, both for me and for those I was assigned to assist. Wherever I went, hands seemed to be reaching out to me for help—for food, for clothes, for medical care, for all the basic necessities of existence.

Through the years I discovered that local churches invariably were unprepared to respond when I approached them for assistance for someone in need nearby—someone who for one reason or another was ineligible for the services provided by city or county or state agencies. Churches might take care of their own, but they seldom reached out to the stranger at their gates. Usually I would not be asking for money— perhaps I would have been given that. No, I would be looking for individual Christians willing to perform temporary acts of caring:

- Christians who would visit the isolated and lonely.
- Christians who would take sick people to doctors.
- Christians who would buy groceries and pre- pare meals.
- Christians who would do a wash and ironing.
- Christians who would baby-sit.
- Christians who would bring friendship and a willing hand to the elderly.
- Christians who could be advocates of the poor and needy.
- Christians who would be 'family' in a society where families are ceasing to exist.

Attitudes toward the care of the young, the old, the sick, or the disadvantaged have altered dramatical- ly since World War II. Commitment to family life seems to be dying. Neighborliness is disappearing. A sense of belonging, of community, is a thing of the past for vast numbers of people who no longer have any ties that connect them with the love and concern of other human beings. There is an urgent need for surrogate or extended families.

Sociologists describe an extended family as one that consists of a large group of persons united by ties of blood or marriage or adoption, usually a group of brothers or sisters and their families presided over by a patriarch or strong father figure. It can be quite elastic. Responsibility for the young or old or sick or troubled is assumed by everyone.

In a sense, the church is God's extended family in the world. The heavenly Father is its patriarch. Our elder brother is Christ, the firstborn among many brethren (Rom. 8:29). The relationship we have with the Father through him is by blood—the precious blood of Christ, by marriage—the church is the bride of Christ, and by adoption—for when the fulness of time was come, God sent forth his Son, born of a woman, born under the law, that we might receive the adoption of sons (Gal. 4:4–5). His love extends to the whole world and he always is seeking those who have not yet become part of his family. When he tells us to love our neighbors as ourselves, he is giving us the opportunity to be like himself.

The amazing thing about God's love is that it is not exclusive. In the Old Testament he repeatedly instructs his people, Israel, to care for the stranger and the sojourner. In Deuteronomy 10:18–19 we read: "He defends the cause of the fatherless and the widow, and loves the alien [stranger], giving him food and clothing. And you are to love those who are aliens, for you yourselves were aliens in Egypt." Numbers 15:16 commands, "The same laws and regulations will apply both to you and to the alien living among you." In the New Testament we are told to do good to all (Gal. 6:10). Christ makes it so clear. The Father in heaven causes his sun to rise on the evil and on the good, and sends rain on the just and on the unjust (Matt. 5:45). If we love only those who love us, what credit is that to us (Luke 6:23)? We are to be merciful as God is merciful (Luke 6:36). Love your enemies, do good to them—then you will be sons of the Most High, because He is kind to the ungrateful and the wicked (Luke 6:35).

Is this the kind of love your church is radiating in the neighborhood where it stands? People today are looking to the church for much more than spiritual help. Are you picking up on their distress signals? How well do you know the community around your church? Are there elderly people living there all alone? Are there others with a disability or a handicap? What about the children? Do youngsters come home to an empty house because parents work all day? Who is ill, who is bereaved, who struggles with alcoholism or drug addiction? What about the unemployed? Do they have food to eat, clothes to wear? Are there some who are straining to learn and understand our language? Is anyone on parole or recently released from prison?

If you don't have the answers to these questions, you are not alone. Most Christians do not. It isn't that we don't care. I am convinced that when we fail to respond to hurting people in our local community it is because we lack exposure, training, and meaningful support systems. We have no plan of action that can become operative, like a volunteer fire department, when a need arises. Like Elijah of old, we have failed to call out God's reserves. We have not developed a strategy of service.

. . . — — — . . .

Four

Looking Back, Looking Ahead

From New Testament times down to the last century, Christians have been characterized by their loving, personal service to the poor, the sick, or the troubled. They were the pioneers of today's social and health services. Three-quarters of the charitable work done in Britain in the nineteenth century is said to have been the work of evangelical Christians. Unfortunately, the world does not tabulate or keep track of our past good deeds. It focuses on our present failures. It has been in our own century, with its great technological and social changes, that the church has relinquished its leadership in ministries to people in crisis. It allowed the major part of this responsibility to be assumed by secular and governmental agencies—agencies that have become so massive, so complex, that individuals seeking help often feel dehumanized, served by a machine rather than by other persons like themselves. Attempts to alleviate human suffering have been made without reference to the greatest need of all, our need for a Savior.

But at long last the pendulum is swinging back. President Reagan, for the first time in American history, gathered representatives of all major religious denominations to a meeting at the White House. He challenged church leaders to become involved again in human service ministries.

No wonder! With our government staggering under a trillion dollar debt, massive economic cutbacks are curtailing the delivery of human services drastically. Even our sacrosanct Social Security system teeters on the brink of bankruptcy. Secular and governmental agencies are totally incapable of meeting the skyrocketing demand for human services. From the White House down to grass-roots America the search is on for people who will give their time and effort sacrificially and in practical ways. The church has the greatest potential for response to the SOS of our own hour.

· · ·   — — —   · · ·

Five

Journey Out of Bitterness

The church has the greatest potential for response. But in my day-to-day experience I find local churches unprepared to respond. They are not disinterested. Expressions of concern, of warm sympathy, usually precede an unsuccessful attempt by the pastor to rally volunteers to meet a specific need. Then, with regret, the minister will tell me that no one can be found who feels able to help at this time or in this situation.

Seldom do churches project indifference. I have encountered only three such instances. One involved a sixteen-year-old named Danny. He was referred for psychological evaluation because he was "acting out" in his foster home. I was sent to assess the situation before he was seen in the clinic. The boy had only one request. He wanted to finish high school. Because of a permanent disability resulting from an illness earlier in the year, his request was being denied. Instead, he had been placed in a rural foster home where he shared a basement room with an elderly stroke victim who could not speak. Like any teenager under similar circumstances, Danny rebelled. Never have I seen such a fighting spirit! And he needed every ounce of grit that he possessed. Deprived of the help of parents or family, his future looked dark indeed.

After Danny was seen at the clinic, a very sensitive psychiatrist came to me. "Willie," he said, "I want you to step out of your role as social worker and be family for this boy. Otherwise, we will lose him." He further recommended that Danny be housed in the city, that the department of education find a way for Danny to complete high school, and that socialization with young people his own age be secured. Housing and education we arranged. But socialization? That which should have been easy proved almost unobtainable.

I went from church to church and from individual to individual, trying to connect with a youth group or persons who would include a boy with a disability in their outings and get-togethers. One woman confided that it was embarrassing to have someone around who was "different." At his high school, he was turned down by a Christian social club because, "Danny doesn't say thank you when somebody helps him. He isn't grateful." Overcoming insurmountable odds, this boy earned his high school diploma, then went on to university for two years. A college charismatic group took him to their hearts at last. The churches never did.

Bobby was six when his mother brought him to the diagnostic center. Something about him was reminiscent of a semi-tame little animal, his shy eagerness for affection straining through his ready-to-run wariness. Physically, he was a handsome youngster with a bright face and glowing eyes. Yet mentally and emotionally he lagged far behind other children his age. His speech especially concerned his mother. It just hadn't developed beyond baby talk. The battery of tests ordered by the specialists seemed too bewildering for Bobby and his mother. After a few failed attempts, I went along with them to the clinics and outpatient departments. The doctors wanted X-rays of his skull, but Bobby couldn't comprehend why he had to stand still with his head held in a certain position against that strange metal contraption. He twisted from his mother's restraining grasp repeatedly.

"Bobby," I said, "We want to take your picture. Did your Daddy ever take your picture with his camera? Remember how you had to stand very still until the camera clicked? This is like that. The doctor wants to take your picture. I'll stand right here with you, with my hands on your head so you'll remember not to move. Then, just before the camera clicks, I'll take my hands away so they won't spoil the picture, okay?"

The intensity of his effort to cooperate surprised me. His little body quivered and his breath came in tiny gasps, but he held still through that long moment when I had to take my hands away. Then he looked up with anxious, yearning expression. It said without words, "Did I do it right this time?" When I hugged him close and praised him, he did a wriggling dance of delight. Surely, I thought, someone with love and skill could reach down inside Bobby to help him.

When all the test results were in, the diagnostic team was not encouraging. Perhaps if Bobby went to a special school, he could be taught. But there were no special classes in the town where he lived. Still, there was a chance. If we could find transportation for him to a town six miles away where there was such a school, he would be accepted for admission. Bobby's parents were too poor to own a car, and there were no buses. I proceeded to knock on every door of every official who might be able to provide a ride for Bobby. Alas, the school was in a different county. Neither county could or would cross their boundary line. In desperation I turned to the churches. Would they organize a car pool? One by one they found reasons to say no. Eventually, the pastor of an active evangelical church assured me that his congregation would provide the service. A week later he called. "I never dreamed it would be so difficult to find people for this," he confessed. "Give me a few more days." Finally he did succeed in persuading a few Christians to set up a car pool. It lasted one week. Then I had another phone call from him. He was outraged.

"We're not driving that kid another day. Do you know what he did? He peed on the people in the back seat of the car!"

That evening when I could think coherently, I wondered how the minister would have reacted if the child had been his grandson instead of Bobby. I wondered if he had entertained the slightest recollection that his Lord let himself be spit upon, mocked, and beaten. Perhaps for Jesus' sake, a Christian could even consent to be peed upon. Possibly in that one glorious act of contempt Bobby revealed the mind of God regarding our crumbs of charity.

Finally, there was Shelby, another six-year-old. Shelby was reported to me for truancy. As the school social worker, it was my job to find her and bring her to school. That wasn't an easy task. Shelby was a black child who lived in a shanty town at one end of the city. Going from shack to shack asking directions, I eventually located the hovel where she had last been seen.

Inside I found her mother in bed, several men seated or lounging at her bedside. Shelby crouched in a corner of the room. "Why wasn't she in school?" I asked. "No shoes, and maybe chicken pox," was the reply. Since there was no evidence of rash and the child had on plastic boots, I took her along to school, stopping enroute to buy shoes and socks. But the truancy continued. Whenever I went in search of her, I would find her in a different location.

Bit by bit I learned the sordid details. Her mother was a prostitute for both men and women. Her father was in the penitentiary. School social workers had brought this family to the attention of the juvenile court repeatedly, asking for foster homes for the children. There were no foster homes for black children. Finally, I tried. The judge, impatient and brusque, cut me short.

"You want her? You can have her. Find a family for her if you can." It was as though he were handing me a sack of meal.

We found a Christian black couple willing to add one more child to their own five. Since the city refused to contribute anything toward Shelby's support, I searched for other sources of assistance. Again I turned to church groups. Would they be willing to help sponsor Shelby? No. Their mission programs for the year were already finalized. They had enough "projects." One Christian friend supplied clothes and five dollars per month for the child. It was the kindness of five other Christians who lived in other parts of the country that provided for Shelby's physical and dental needs. Over half her baby teeth were abscessed.

At the end of a year, her pediatrician said, "Physically she has improved 100 per cent. Mentally and emotionally? Only time will tell. It takes years to overcome such a beginning. Some never make it."

Shelby was one who didn't make it. When she was in her teens a social worker thought it would be nice to reunite the original family briefly to see if healing could occur. By this time, I had moved to another area. That one reunion was Shelby's undoing. The last I heard she was on the street, her mother pimping for her. Christian friends were quick to write to me about it. Yet none of them went to her, as they would have if it had been their own child, to try to win her back.

These are extreme cases, but they forced me out of my complacent misconception about the local church. Like most Christians—and non-Christians—I had falsely assumed that churches have a plan for the unplanned, a thought-out strategy of response to an unexpected SOS. That this is not so is a sad fact that can be documented by anyone who works in the field of human services. In time I began to react to this disappointment with anger and indignation. It hurt me when unbelievers among my professional peers smiled and shrugged if I suggested that a local church could be a source of comfort and encouragement and help. Most of them had explored that possibility and experienced the same letdown I had. I became almost as disillusioned as they.

Fortunately, God did not abandon me to bitterness. He led me to Hawaii for a few years. There in the Aloha State I discovered a church with a loose-knit organization called a Shepherds' Society. It was set up to deal with any crisis that might occur among the people of the congregation—a plan for the unplanned. If a member became ill or faced an emergency, the shepherds who lived nearby were alerted. They would visit the one in need to work out a care plan involving as many shepherds as necessary. It was a simple arrangement, but it worked well. There were no paid personnel, just concerned lay Christians who accepted the referrals made by their ministers and others in the congregation.

This experience taught me the value and necessity of having a plan of action, an operational procedure. To be effective, this kind of ministry needs strategy and structure.

The minister and the missions committee wanted the service to be made available to those outside the congregation, to those in the surrounding community. But this the Shepherds' Society flatly refused to consider. When I asked for an explanation the leader confessed, "We're afraid! We're afraid we'll be asked to do something we won't be able to handle!"

This experience also taught me to be aware of the paralyzing power of fear and of the importance of training for this kind of ministry.

I remembered how frightened I was when I first began to work in the community as a Maternity Center nurse. How carefully the other nurses prepared me and accompanied me until I gained confidence. Why should I expect church people to feel any less timid than I did when faced with an unfamiliar task?

And at that point it seemed as if the Lord were tapping me on the shoulder to do something about training Christians for neighborhood ministries.

· · — — — · ·

Six

Seminary—the Long and the Short of It

When the Holy Spirit plants an idea in the mind, it usually is followed up by marching orders. Mine came in the form of a young man with a seminary catalog under his arm. Bob was about to enter the ministry. As I leafed through his booklet, I noted one particular program description—"Urban Ministries Emphasis." Partly in jest I asked, "Bob, would the seminary admit a woman my age?" He looked dubious. "I don't know. I have heard that there are more women accepted every year." I scratched down the address of the school, never seriously believing I would receive an encouraging answer. A few months later, at the age of fifty, I was on my way to seminary.

My goal was not ordination. I did not feel called to a preaching ministry. Nor was it theological education, primarily. I was on a fact-finding mission. I wanted to know why local churches fail in servanthood. I wanted to know how to reverse this trend. Surely a seminary would have some answers.

Instead of being enlightened by the seminary

experience, I found myself engulfed in a tidal wave of theology and theory. There was little that focused on the practicalities of preparing believers for tangible forms of service in their own communities. Involving lay Christians in the liturgical worship within the church itself was the chief focus of the seminary. I couldn't believe my ears. Didn't these learned professors realize that the man or the woman on the street doesn't give a hoot about who reads the Scriptures at the Sunday morning service or who serves communion? What they do care about is, "I was sick, I was lonely, I was hungry, I was in prison and you didn't care about me." That's the church's biggest black eye.

Over the next several years, taking advantage of cross-registration opportunities in master of divinity and doctor of ministry programs, I attended classes in eleven different seminaries in the Boston area and in Chicago. I studied the curriculum of each school, conversed with students, assessed the emphasis of each program. At least part of the answer to my question about servanthood became apparent: seminaries do not prepare pastors to equip lay Christians with the skills and confidence essential to this aspect of ministry. Theologians deal with weightier matters— hermeneutics, exegesis, eschatology, doctrine, ancient languages, the historic faith. How to be a good neighbor, the kind Jesus talked about, apparently is just too simple for seminaries. The theology of poverty was examined painstakingly. How to feed the hungry family next door scarcely got a nod.

Every class and every assignment became my opportunity to reiterate that the saints need to be trained for community service ministries as for all others. It is not enough to preach stirring sermons about the Good Samaritan. The "how-to" has to be demonstrated. Frequently other students came to me

with questions and requests: "May I have a copy of
the paper you presented in class?" "Would you tell
me more about how to get a service ministry started in
my church?" "Why don't we learn these things here at
seminary?"

Most of these young people were assigned to
various churches for field work. When confronted by
human grief and calamity, they could minister to
spiritual needs, but they were ill-equipped to deal in
practicalities.

James 2:16 asks, "Suppose a brother or sister is
without clothes and daily food. If one of you says to
him, 'Go, I wish you well; keep warm and well fed,'
but does nothing about his physical needs, what good
is it?"

Sensitive to the Word of God, many seminary
students feel that they are being short-changed during
their years of preparation. As one of them so aptly put
it when faced by the urgent needs of a dispossessed
family, "What in my seminary program prepares me
for this?"

Thank God, two clinical experiences redeemed
those frustrating theological years for me. One professor wanted us to know how transient or runaway
teenagers feel when they get off a bus in a strange city
where no one knows them and where they do not
wish to be known. We were instructed to report to our
first class in our oldest, warmest clothes—it was winter
in Boston—and to carry only fifty cents and a
handkerchief in our pockets. With minimal direction
we were turned out into the cold to fend for ourselves.
For three days and two nights we were to find food,
shelter, and if possible, temporary employment. We
were to try to keep our true identity a secret.

I was the only older person in the class. I couldn't
pass myself off as a teenager. The best I could do was

to look and to act pathetic, which was about the way I felt. It was late in the afternoon when we hit the streets. I was terrified at the prospect of spending the night out of doors in that tough neighborhood. Twenty-five years of work in the slums didn't prepare me to be stranded overnight on skid row.

Where does a homeless woman of my age go in a city if she is avoiding the authorities—the police and others who might ask questions? My only idea was to make a bee-line for the nearest Salvation Army center, a place called the Harbor Light. Could they give me food and a place to sleep for a few nights, I pleaded. To my dismay I learned that all their beds for women were already assigned. Mercifully, a case worker arranged for me to sleep two nights at a nearby Roman Catholic haven sponsored by the Legion of Mary. I could have breakfast there and evening meals at the Harbor Light. Very few questions were asked. At bedtime a large cardboard box filled with unironed but clean pajamas and nightgowns was brought out. I selected something to sleep in. There was a shower and soap. But oh for a toothbrush and deodorant! The first night I was the only one in the room where I slept. At midnight the second night, a young woman slipped into the other bed. We said "Good night" and "Good morning." That was all. The whole experience was kept painlessly anonymous.

Between 9:00 A.M. and 5:00 P.M., I roamed the streets or passed time in the public library or in churches that were open. The necessities of life narrowed down to a precious few: warmth, water to drink, and a free bathroom. For the first time I noticed how many chairs in the library were occupied by shabbily dressed street people hiding behind newspapers. Some slept as they held an open book. As long as they were quiet, no one disturbed them. I found many women my age and older seeking shelter—battered women, elderly and confused women, physically and mentally ill women, drug-addicted women. All were impoverished. All were desperately afraid that no place would be found for them—that they would be left out on the streets for the night.

I thought about them as I sat in a warm corner of the sanctuary of one of Boston's leading churches. I looked at that vast expanse of cushioned pews, wondering how many people could be bedded down there. I wondered if that congregation knew that only a few blocks away there were scores of people with no place to lay their heads.

Later in the year I returned to the Harbor Light and to the Legion of Mary Home. Acknowledging my true identity, I asked what church people could do to help. In both places the answer was the same: "If small groups of Christians would befriend just one or two abandoned persons—keep tabs on them, see that they have received their checks, have paid their rent, and have taken their medication—and give them practical, loving supervision, it would contribute immensely to their safety, their sanity, and perhaps to their salvation."

My most rewarding experience while at seminary consisted of a summer of field work in Chicago. A Roman Catholic nun introduced me to a program called Parish Community Services.

"We're doing the very thing you are talking about," she said. "Would you like to see the manual we use when we train our lay people?"

She went on to explain that during Vatican II it was mandated that every Catholic parish must develop some plan or procedure whereby those in need in the surrounding community may be served.

Overcoming my strong, evangelical Protestant

bias, I investigated this program being sponsored by Catholic Charities of Chicago. All over that city, without fanfare or publicity, Catholic lay people have banded together to serve in the neighborhoods around their churches. The training they receive is very basic and not highly technical. The goal is to allay fears and to build confidence. It includes a review of communication skills, simple interviewing techniques, practice in setting up a plan of action with someone in distress, a grasp of the major community resources and how to be an advocate for those using them. Service is seen as an integral part of their worshiping experience, a continuation of the work of Christ through the life of each caring person. Prayer and sharing are woven into every aspect of this loving outreach effort.

During my eight weeks of field work with Parish Community Services, I was rotated from parish to parish throughout the city and suburbs in widely divergent ethnic, racial, and economic situations. I visited all black communities, Hispanic neighborhoods, areas in transition, and affluent and stable sections of the city. I sat in on volunteer training sessions, accompanied volunteers on their assignments, and attended their sharing sessions afterwards. These Catholic care-persons took on all kinds of grassroots ministries. They prepared meals for the home bound, ran errands, did chores, provided transportation, wrote letters, filled out forms, acted as advocates, gave personal care, read aloud, and prayed, sang, and shared the Word of God. They were family to those who often were strangers to them, people of every faith or of no faith at all. There was very little that they could not or would not do, and all without any charge whatsoever.

The difference between these programs being

sponsored by the Catholic Church and those of most Protestant churches is that they have a definite plan of action that includes training for service. When we are intentional about our caring, when we have "a plan for the unplanned"—for the needs of those who live outside our society's plan—people in need are less apt to be overlooked, and no single care-person bears too much of the burden. These Catholic Christians have a strategy of service.

· · · — — —   · · ·

Seven

Growing Pains

I took the knowledge and skills acquired in Chicago and experimented with them in Protestant circles. My first attempt involved a large evangelical church renowned for its support of foreign and home missions.

"I am afraid you won't find many who will be interested," confided one of the ministers. "Our people are marvelous when it comes to giving for missions, but they don't volunteer readily for tasks that involve them personally."

Nevertheless, we scheduled a Saturday workshop. At the senior pastor's request, two representatives from every level, beginning with the trustees and deacons and ending with the senior highs, were present. Twenty of us spent that Saturday morning exploring the whole concept of the church as servant. We reviewed the biblical mandates, the example of Christ and the early Christians. Then, with our Lord's words fresh in our minds, we fanned out two by two into the surrounding city, asking ourselves again the question, "Who is my neighbor?"

We explored the residential area near the church. We covered bus terminals, train depots, subway stations, hospital emergency rooms, fast-food retaurants, markets in poverty areas, parks and public gathering places, "downtown", the combat zone. Reassembling at the end of the afternoon, we prayed together and then brainstormed over our evening meal.

The minister of visitation reported that he had a list of two hundred infirm or home-bound people whom he attempted to visit briefly every month. How he would welcome help with that ministry! Having spent a day with him on his rounds, I could appreciate his desperate need of assistance. Another clergy member spoke of the increasing number of street people coming to the church door for aid. Could some of their needs be met by lay Christians?

The enthusiastic response of the group exceeded all expectation. Each one present agreed to go back to those he or she represented, to report on our experiences and to encourage others to join them in attending four training sessions I was prepared to teach. Out of that nucleus, in a church where people "do not volunteer," more than seventy Christians pledged themselves to specific service ministries at least once a month. They were asked to make realistic commitments. We urged monthly assignments, faithfully performed, rather than weekly commitments not carried out.

These Christians were far from reluctant. They seemed grateful for a chance to serve in personal, practical ways. And the response of those whom they served was gratifying. College students, especially, merited the praise of the elderly. One young couple assumed responsibility for watching over the house and yard of a hospitalized woman. When she came home, they did her marketing. Another college boy carried boxes up from the cellar for an older person who could no longer climb stairs. She had been wanting to look through those boxes for months but couldn't get to them. Simple kindness, yes, but what a boost to those involved!

A retired nurse who had lost her eyesight needed people to read and converse with her. She lived alone in her apartment. We linked her with several volunteers then watched in awe as her own ministry expanded. No one who went to her door came away unblessed. Her courage, optimism, humor, and generousity far outshone anything we attempted on her behalf. Her genius for friendship touched my life in so positive a way that I thank God for her every day.

With a membership of over two thousand, this church drew worshipers from a large area. It was a regional church. By dividing the region into several smaller sections, we were able to match those in need with volunteers who lived closest to them. All went well until my studies took me to another part of the country. Who would direct the volunteer service, make assignments, and coordinate the work of laity with that of clergy when I left? I had neglected one of the most critical aspects of lay ministry. I had failed to train lay leaders.

The responsibility of my work fell on the shoulders of an already overburdened mission worker whose other priorities took precedence. Within a year the service ministry that had been so promising dwindled and died. The plaintive letters I received from many of the volunteers asking why they no longer were being given assignments, wondering why the program had been discontinued, forced me to look at the facts. In a church with at least six ministers, it failed for lack of leadership. It was a costly and painful way to learn that I had not yet developed an effective strategy of service.

· · ·   — — —   · · ·

Eight

Clustering Churches to Network a Neighborhood

I tried again. This time I elected to work with six churches in a more circumscribed geographic area. Would they share concerns and consolidate efforts to serve those in need around them?

A distinct disadvantage had surfaced during my previous attempt with a single church. We were not meshing our efforts with those of other churches around us. We had no way of knowing whether we were duplicating services or overlooking unmet needs. It is unlikely that one church can discover or respond to all the emergency human needs in its community, but a cluster of churches might network a neighborhood quite successfully.

The theological justification for such an attempt relates to Christ's prayer in John 17:21, "That all of them may be one." The concept of the church as one body, joined and knit together in love, motivated my effort (Rom. 12:8; I Cor. 12:12–26; Eph. 4:1–16). Yet I realized that centuries of theological differences and denominational separateness could very effectively doom such an attempt. In this twentieth century could we at least share information and coordinate our service ministries in a specific locality?

I chose Chicago for this attempt because of the head start my field work had given me there. One section of the city was very familiar to me. During my summer of field work, the Parish Community Services coordinator and I had visited a number of churches in that area to acquaint pastors with the availability of this neighborhood ministry. The groundwork for a cluster had already been done.

My immediate objectives were:

- To find six churches of various denominations that would be willing to participate in a cluster project.
- To conduct four training sessions in each of these churches.
- To obtain from the pastors a list of names of people who would need the helping services and skills that would be developed through the training sessions.
- To set up monthly cluster meetings, bringing together the six church groups to share experiences, to exchange knowledge of the neighborhood, to support one another in worship and fellowship, and to facilitate both cross-referrals and coordinated efforts.

On foot and by bus, with map in hand, I explored that section of Chicago. I noted every church in the area. Then I singled out six—a Methodist, a Presbyterian, a Baptist, a Lutheran, a United Church of Christ, and a Roman Catholic. My first step in attempting to cluster these churches was to enlist the support and cooperation of the clergy. The pastor is the key person in any church organizational change. Without pastoral backing, clustering would be impossible. I developed a clergy support base at the onset.

From the start God's leading was evident in a very delightful way. The first minister I approached was the pastor of the Baptist church. I had met him during my field work the summer before. In our preliminary small talk he mentioned that he grew up in Albert County, New Brunswick. That was a name I recognized. My mother was from Albert County, New Brunswick. When I next talked to her on the phone, I mentioned him. Immediately interested, she asked me to find out if he was related to a particular family in the tiny village in New Brunswick where she had spent her childhood. To make a long story short, we discovered that our family tree and his family tree had merged several times, beginning as far back as the seventeen hundreds! The genealogies flew back and forth between my mother and the pastor's sister. Talk about a small world! Or rather, talk about a great God who led me to the one minister, of all the clergy in Chicago, who was "kinfolk!" I became known as "Cousin Willie" in that Baptist church. "Cousin Bob" threw his wholehearted support behind the cluster. He accompanied me personally when I visited the pastors of the other churches. All agreed to be part of the cluster. Later another Catholic church asked to be included.

Note that there was no price tag on my services. The response might have been very different if there had been. As a doctoral student I was the recipient of a grant that covered my living expenses. I was able to coordinate the cluster for a year without charge.

The second step involved meeting the lay leadership in the five Protestant churches. The pastors set up opportunities for me to talk to deacons, elders, councils, or committees about the cluster concept. I shared my image of the church as the body of Christ and my understanding of ministry, relating it to the servanthood of Jesus and the priesthood of all believers. This fit in with the values, goals, traditions, and expectations of those to whom I spoke. The response was positive. They were willing to give their support and to encourage others in the congregation to participate. In the two Catholic churches, where training had been given by Parish Community Services of Catholic Charities, lay volunteer groups already existed. Their coordinators prepared them for participation in the cluster.

I spent a summer familiarizing myself with the human service resources of the community and its needs. After twenty-five years in public health and social services I know that every community and every church has its lonely, its ill, its destitute. I counted on clergy to put us in touch with such people who were known to them. I felt that a detailed assessment was best left until the cluster Christians themselves were motivated to initiate and carry it out.

In August the pastors of the cluster churches met to synchronize the scheduling and publicizing of a series of four sixty-minute training sessions I would teach in September. I purposely taught in each of the five Protestant churches separately. Group cohesiveness and a mutual support factor are essential for success. If I had gathered together one large group from all the churches, it would have been composed of people who were at best only newly acquainted. The concept of clustering was presented to each small group frequently so that it was a familiar idea long before any clustering occurred.

We attempted to set up the weekly training sessions in conjunction with ongoing church activities, taking over timeslots usually filled by regularly scheduled programs, for example, the Sunday school hour, the Sunday evening fellowship hour, or the midweek service time. In this way we could avoid asking people to return to the church for an additional day or evening. The classes were publicized so as to interest anyone who wanted to learn more about the needs of the community and how to meet them. That was not frightening or threatening. I wanted to train as many as would come before attempting any recruitment. I wanted people to understand exactly what was involved before I made an effort to enlist them for service.

Those who attended were marvelously supportive. The groups were small, no more than twenty-four in attendance at any one gathering. At the final session I gave everyone the opportunity to sign a commitment form, pledging themselves to specific service ministries once a month. Practically everyone found something on that check list that they were willing to do. (See appendix 1.)

Each church developed its own group of volunteers with its own name—The Shepherds, Helping Hands, Caring and Sharing, etc. A card file was set up at each site, listing alphabetically the names of the volunteers in that church, then categorized according to task commitment. A third section in the file contained the names of those requiring services. (See appendix 2.) Referrals initially came from clergy and from church members. Later they came from outside agencies as well.

The volunteers in each church agreed to meet once a month to receive their assignments and to report on the person that they had last served. Before the first monthly meeting at the Baptist church, a noticeable degree of timidity developed. Although many had attended the training sessions and had responded favorably, it became apparent that as the day of actual service approached, there was increasing reluctance on the part of many.

I discussed this with Cousin Bob on the Sunday morning that first assignments were to be made. He picked up on it immediately and devoted part of his sermon time to acquainting the congregation with those who were about to engage in this new venture of faith and ministry. He recognized all the Christian care-persons by name, asking them to rise one by one. When the worship service ended and the volunteers made their way to the room where they would receive their first assignments, the difference was remarkable. It was as though they marched to flutes and drums and bugles. All reluctance had disappeared. Every assignment was accepted and carried out.

Each month thereafter, on communion Sunday, they met to report to one another, to seek guidance, and to take on new service ministries. The sensitive, spontaneous action of the pastor was crucial to this success. Without his strong support the whole venture might have failed.

In many ways Cousin Bob's church was the testing ground for each development that then would be introduced to the other cluster churches. A very concise form of recording was worked out. The briefest of notes regarding the current status of the people served was added to the card file each month. My purpose was to train competent Christians, not incompetent social workers. Records and statistics, the two bugaboos of Parish Community Services volunteers, were kept minimal in the cluster. A one-page check list clearly displayed the service record of each volunteer for twelve months. (See appendix 3.)

Simplicity had to be the name of the game.

Confidential matters were not recorded. An unlocked file box in an open church is no place for intimate details. Two of the group, a registered nurse and a deaconess, assumed responsibility for the card file at the Baptist church and for presiding over the monthly meetings. The minister and I were present as resource people. This pattern was duplicated in the the other cluster groups. It was not adhered to precisely or exactly. Each group made modifications and adapted the process to its own purposes.

In October the crucial step of networking was at hand. The Baptists offered to host the first cluster meeting. The clergy in each church announced the event from their pulpits and included it in church calendars. Posters about the cluster appeared on bulletin boards.

The first meeting was a time for getting acquainted and for planning. Each church group agreed to host one cluster meeting in the coming months and to be responsible for its program. The cluster operated without a budget. Each church chose speakers who would give their time and talent without charge. Advantage was taken of the many resource people available to us without cost from various community agencies. Within the cluster itself were those who were able to share knowledge and skills.

The meetings were meant to provide ongoing service-oriented education, focusing on the surrounding community, as well as opportunity for worship and sharing. Some time was allotted at each meeting for discussion so that volunteers could tell about their experiences, their frustrations, and successes. Soon the trust level developed to the extent that cross-referrals were being made among the cluster churches. When necessary a combined effort enabled the cluster

to meet needs that one church alone would not have
been able to service.

Each meeting followed a similar format, not
because it was required, but because it seemed to be a
familiar, comfortable style. Several volunteers stood
outside the church to direct traffic to the proper
entrance and room. Two other volunteers were
responsible for the sign-in sheet. They saw that
everyone had a nametag. A welcome would be
extended to all, both by the presiding layperson and
by the pastor of the hosting church. An opening
prayer, followed by a portion of Scripture, was next.
Again, both laity and clergy might share in this
function. Music was a favorite part of every cluster
meeting. Song sheets, guitars, hymnals, quartets, even
choirs were brought in. Hymns familiar to both
Catholics and Protestants were searched out or new
choruses were learned.

After the singing, announcements were made by
the presiding layperson. Comments from the audience
were encouraged. People felt free to speak out, to
question, to interrupt. The topics and speakers for the
evening were selected and invited by the host group,
based on the interests expressed by the whole cluster
at its first meeting. I was available for consultation and
collaboration, but increasingly, as the groups gained
confidence, my input was needed less and less. A time
of informal mixing and socializing concluded each
meeting. Refreshments were supplied by the host
church.

At the end of one cluster meeting a woman
commented, "I forget entirely that I'm not with just my
own church group. We all seem to be one."

Walls began to come down, communication was
enhanced, spiritual and physical needs were being met
by this small group of churches working through a

network in their own neighborhood. Clergy people who formerly served in the community without knowing one another became acquainted. Their relationships took on a mutual helpfulness and respect. The participants focused on our faith in Christ, not on our differences. No one had any quarrel, theologically, with our strategy of service.

The development of lay leadership paralleled the cluster meetings. During the four training sessions I had prayerfully assessed the leadership potential in each group. Seeking God's guidance, I selected two from each church to become part of the planning, directing heart of the cluster, the Cluster Core. The pastors and I agreed that we should serve as resource people, providing backup but not leadership. I would coordinate the effort only until the Cluster Core could take over. Our goal was to place leadership functions in the hands of the laity as rapidly as their skills allowed.

The two persons from each church were not only planners, but linking persons, who would link the volunteers in their own church with the rest of the congregation on the one hand, then link that church and its volunteers with the cluster on the other hand. I did not make the choice of the Cluster Core membership a group decision. Prayerfully, depending on the Holy Spirit for guidance, I selected and appointed twelve, as Jesus did his disciples. They proved trustworthy—strong links that held.

In early December at our first Cluster Core meeting, I transferred leadership into their hands. In all honesty, the transition was too abrupt. I had not prepared them sufficiently. They seemed bewildered, but they did not grumble or protest or complain. They rose to the occasion and valiantly tried. I realized at the very first cluster meeting under their leadership that I had neglected to equip them with basic skills, such as how to open a meeting, how to get the attention of the audience, how to introduce a speaker, how to lead a discussion, how to close. They learned these things the hard way, on their feet, in front of the cluster.

I had operated under the false assumption that they already possessed rudimentary skills that would enable them to do all these things. Some were more experienced or gifted than others. A few were so nervous they literally trembled, their voices shook. Most of them had been active in their churches for years but they had been behind-the-scene workers. They were much more at ease serving the refreshments than leading the meeting or offering a public prayer. To thrust leadership responsibilities upon them two months after they completed the four basic training sessions was premature. Yet it did result in lay leadership, uncertain and unskilled initially, but increasingly confident and competent as time passed.

Gently advised by their pastors that they would provide support and encouragement but not leadership, cut off from dependence on myself, the original coordinator, the Cluster Core squared its collective shoulders and assumed command. That it managed to survive, that it reached its decisions by consensus, witnesses to the commitment of these Cluster Core Christians. One member agreed to be the chairperson. Every year or two this office was to be filled by another, and half of the Cluster Core was to be replaced by other cluster members. It was hoped that this would result in a shared leadership that would not be dominated by any one person or any one church.

The cluster has been a low-key operation. Yet, like a volunteer fire department, these Christians are prepared to respond when a need arises. At one point, during a severe winter, the coordinator of a Meals on

Wheels program made an emergency appeal to the cluster for more drivers. The response was immediate and the service was able to carry on. Another call came for daily transportation to and from the hospital for six weeks for an elderly woman receiving laser beam treatment. By rallying the whole cluster and asking for a combined effort, rides were provided. The cluster looked into a report that there were people in nursing homes in the surrounding community who never had visitors, either having outlived their families or having been abandoned by them. Several of the cluster groups "adopted" residents recommended by the homes. While providing friendship they have become familiar with one particular facility. They are able to relay information about it to the cluster as a whole.

As my school year ended I realized that the pressures of study and other commitments had kept me from a number of very important considerations. I never explored with the cluster the possibility of a door-to-door assesssment of the community. Neither had I stressed ongoing recruitment. Cluster Christians had been faithfully committed to their fellowship of service, but they had not made a deliberate effort to enlist others to become involved.

More than four years have passed since the cluster began functioning. Whenever my travels take me through Chicago, I call one of the Cluster Core for an update. At last report the cluster continued to be in operation. How long will it survive? It will not live forever. There is a life-cycle for every group and for every program, just as there is for every individual.

Shortly after finishing my work with the cluster, I was asked by a seminary in Chicago to teach a course: "Enabling Lay Leadership for Community Service." I invited the Cluster Core to conduct one class. I will never forget that session. Their confidence and their ability to hold the attention of their audience thrilled me. They had a story to tell, and I wish every seminarian could have heard it. They explained that they had found a way to reach out to people in distress without adding another professional's salary to their already strained church budgets. They had discovered anew that many hands make light work. Through shared leadership and short-term commitments they were ministering to their community themselves. By clustering their churches they were networking their neighborhoods. They had a strategy of service.

· · · — — — · · ·

Nine

Clues for Clergy

The question most often put to me by clergy is, "How do I set up an SOS ministry in my church?" I can sympathize with their uncertainty. Since seminaries shy away from "how-to's," most ministers learn them the hard way, by trial and error—after they leave schools of theology.

I can compare it to a similar dilemma in the field of nursing: From the time of Florence Nightingale, every nurse has been taught the principles of nursing. Anywhere in the world those principles are the same. But as hospitals developed, each devised its own "procedure book"—a how-to manual for those in its employ. As time went on, nurses became tied to the procedure book of their particular hospital. If they moved to a different place, they found it hard to forget the procedures of the hospital where they had been in the past and to learn the procedures of another hospital. Eventually, nursing educators experimented with throwing out the procedure book altogether.

If a professional person learns the principles, that

is supposed to be enough. A procedure can be figured out in each situation, based on those principles. There followed an era of confusion in nursing. Fortunately, the pendulum is swinging back. We need both principle and flexible procedure.

In the history of our own country we see the same pattern. The founding fathers hammered out the principles of our nation for all to see and hear:

> "We hold these truths to be self-evident, that all men are created equal, that they are endowed by their Creator with certain inalienable rights, that among these are life, liberty, and the pursuit of happiness. . . ."

These are the principles that all Americans hold dear. Yet it wasn't long before the founding fathers met again to hammer out the Constitution of the United States of America—the "how-to" manual that, if properly applied, insures the fulfillment of the American dream for every citizen.

The Bible primarily is a book of principles. We get into trouble if we snatch a verse here or a text there and fail to relate it to the whole of God's revealed truth. But fortunately for our finite minds, the Bible has its share of "how-to's" as well, for example, Exodus 18:13–27; Acts 6:1–6; Romans 12–16; Galatians 6; Ephesians 4–6; Philippians 2–4; Colossians 2–4; 1 and 2 Timothy; and most of James. Much of the New Testament is specific material that answers questions the early churches had about procedure.

William E. Harden points out in his book, *A Layman's Guide to Protestant Theology,* that

> "From the Christian viewpoint, theological thinking is not an end in itself, Christianity is to be lived; it is to issue in action; as long as it

remains merely thought it is unchristian and futile. But it is a half-truth because whatever a man does depends upon what he thinks and what he holds of ultimate view." [1]

A lodestar for me is 1 John 2:5b, 6. "This is how we know we are in him: Whoever claims to live in him must walk as Jesus did". In seminary libraries I found a tremendous amount of material on Christian education—what to teach from the cradle to the grave. There was next to nothing that dealt with what I would call clinical training for local community ministry. It has been in my work with churches that the following conclusions [2] have become apparent:

> *To acquire care-skills, Christians need training that involves concrete, progressive experience in order to overcome fear of the unknown.*

Recognize the power of fear and the reluctance and uncertainty that stem from inexperience. Deal with this by basic training in communication skills followed by factual data relating to whatever aspect of service the volunteer has elected. See that training is ongoing, each step building on previous learning. Make assignments in keeping with the stated preference of the care-person, increasing simple assignments to more demanding ones as readiness and willingness are indicated. Encourage a buddy system so that knowledge and experience can be shared, especially on initial assignments. Assure freedom to refuse an assignment. Provide for a resource person or backup system to be available at all times, either through knowledgeable people within the church or by tele-

---

[1]William E. Harden, *A Laymen's Guide to Protestant Theology* (New York: Macmillan, 1968) p. XIV.

[2]Dr. Lynn Rhodes, who served as my major professor and project director at the Boston University School of Theology, gave invaluable assistance in the stating of the conclusions contained in this chapter.

phone access to a community information and referral source. Schedule monthly feedback and reassessment sessions. All these provisions are efforts to overcome fear and to build confidence. They pay off.

> *Lay Christians and clergy need to learn that nonprofessional helpers have their own integrity and skills.*

SOS Christians are not poorly trained social workers or less able than professionals. They have a contribution to make that is uniquely their own, born of the very essence of their humanity and their experience of Christ and of crisis.

Good training will validate the lay person's own experience as a basis for work. It will provide specific skills related to listening and advocacy, the procedures to assess community needs and resources, and the ability to develop a plan of action. It will sharpen organizational skills, promote simplicity of structure, management, and record-keeping through shared leadership. It will regularize the recruitment of new members.

> *Christian care-persons need local church grounding, a community of faith that supports the individual in her/his tasks.*

A closely knit community combined with an interdenominational, interchurch program of service necessitates a deliberate tension. Both are essential for the progressive development of care-persons. It is educationally sound to start with the familiar, to build upon the support system already inherent in the local church family. Within the framework of that security, the group has the capacity to develop a wider vision, to respond to challenges to form networks in their neighborhood by clustering with other Christian care-persons in other churches. The encouragement that springs from each group of Christian care-persons has a binding effect on the members. They bear one another's burdens, pray with and for one another, share common interests and concerns, have a mutual commitment to Christ and to one another. The geographic community in which they function is familiar and circumscribed, thereby reducing fear factors.

Theological and spiritual resources are crucial to maintaining motivation and support.

Christian care-persons see worship as well as education as an essential part of every kind of meeting, no matter how businesslike the occasion. Consistently they reject agendas that crowd or diminish prayer, reflection, and praise. They see themselves as *Christian* care-persons and perceive that the difference between themselves and secular volunteers is their relationship to Christ.

The development of lay leadership relates directly to the perceived function of clergy and/or professionals. When these serve in a supportive capacity, as consultants and resource-people rather than as leaders, laity grow in confidence and skills.

Ephesians 4:11, 12 tells us that the gifts of pastor and teacher are given to equip the saints for the work of ministry, for building up the body of Christ. Pastors sometimes pursue a parental role, forgetting what every wise parent knows: growth and ultimate maturity depend on severing the umbilical cord, on thrusting the fledgling out of the nest. Spiritually, this is the way to maturity, to the measure of the stature of the fulness of Christ.

We are to grow up in every way into him who is the Head, into Christ, from whom the whole body, joined and knit together by every joint with which it is supplied, when each part is working properly, makes bodily growth and upbuilds itself in love (Eph. 4:15, 16). Relinquishment is the greatest service of the pastor.

Call out God's reserves! Entrust a ministry of service to the many gifted ones in your congregation. Be a resource person. Provide support and encouragement, but let others lead. Assume a minor role at SOS meetings. Add the endorsement of your presence, but let others preside, let others offer prayer. If you have a schedule conflict, let the work go on, with or without you.

The SOS ministry deserves a secure position within the overall program and budget of the church.

If a service ministry fits naturally into an already existing structure, for example, as a branch of the mission-action committee, then it may be part of that committee's involvement.

Since preparing lay Christians for service ministries is essentially an educational effort, it seems logical to place training within the framework and budget of the Christian education program of the church.

This is not a parachurch activity. Nor is it the business of a select few. Service is the mandate of the Bible for every believer. Even those in the church who have not taken the training sessions and who do not feel free to accept a once-a-month assignment may be part of an SOS auxiliary and occasionally accompany SOS Christians as they serve in the community.

In a large church it may be possible to have a paid coordinator, but it is not essential. In some cases it may even be detrimental, especially if the coordinator assumes control instead of placing leadership functions in the hands of the laity.

Because the chief responsibility of pastors and teachers in the church is to equip the people for works of service, one of the major roles they can play in service ministry is that of trainer. If they don't do training of members themselves, they can support and assist those who do.

The material contained in the chapters that follow has in view the training needs of Christians who are willing to be servants. It can be taught by any competent Christian, lay or professional. The purpose of this material is to draw out the already existing gifts and skills of the people of God to learn to use and apply what we already know. I am indebted to the Catholic Charities of the Archdiocese of Chicago for their gracious permission to adapt some of the following material from their *Training Manual for Volunteers.*

· · · — — — · · ·

Ten

People Need People

We want to reach out to people who are hurting. How do we begin? I find it valuable to use a little sanctified imagination first of all. When I hurt, what helps me? After all, no one has a franchise on being the helper. Don't we all participate when it comes to pain and failure and sorrow and sin and crisis? Sometimes we give the helping hand. Just as often we are in need of it ourselves. It is a two-way process.

Most of us shrink form the word "client." We want to be a friend and we want to have a friend. If we start out with this in mind, we will have gone a long way toward bridging any gulf that separates us from other human beings. No matter what their circumstances, we are not superior to them. We are sharers. We have something in common with everyone else on earth. We know what it is to be afraid, to hurt.

When I sat in on the Parish Community Services training sessions in Chicago, this was illustrated very graphically. For just a few moments we were asked to close our eyes, to relax. Then we were told to concentrate on a time in our lives when we were in deep distress, to relive it in memory. Next we were instructed to put into one word the feelings we experienced at that time. When we opened our eyes we were asked to call out the words so that they could be written on the blackboard. What a long list of negative, unpleasant emotions! Everyone was thinking of a different experience, yet we all knew what it was like to feel lonely, fearful, anxious, depressed, angry, hostile, betrayed, abandoned.

Through our own unique experience we can understand the feelings of people whose circumstances are unlike anything we ourselves have endured. In this way we can identify with them and share their pain. [1] With only a little training we can help them to seek solutions that are constructive, to find the resources and courage to cope until the crisis ends or until they have the situation under control. We stand by them as Christ, through the Holy Spirit, stands by us. It is when we attempt to meet the felt needs of someone in crisis that we are given the opportunity to witness to our faith in the Lord Jesus, to extend the love and concern of the heavenly Father. We do not force our faith on anyone, but we are sensitive to the Holy Spirit's leading and are ready at any time to give a quiet and reverent answer to anyone who wants a reason for the hope that we have within us (1 Peter 3:15).

One of the first lessons to learn, if we are going to reach out to others, is to call them by the name they prefer. Our names are important to us. Find out if you should use the familiar first name or a nickname or whether, as is sometimes the case with elderly people,

---

[1] Catholic Charities of Chicago, *Training Manual for Volunteers — Catholic Charities Parish Community Services* (Chicago: June 1977), p. 16.

the formal last name is expected. I prefer to be called Willie. It's a nickname from my last name, Williams. It has pleasant associations for me. When someone calls me by my given name, June, it connects me with less positive memories. I hear it in a New England grandmother's voice, "June, tie your shoes," or "June, it's bedtime." I am pleased when you call me Willie.

It was a very different story with my mother. She considered it disrespectful if any younger person addressed her with familiarity. A few years ago at the age of 87, she was rushed to the hospital, hemorrhaging from a gastric ulcer. One of the young nurses in the intensive care unit who was working frantically to save my mother's life spoke to her, calling her by her first name, "Edith." Even at death's door my mother lifted her head from the pillow and said in a weak but determined voice, "Mrs. Williams, please." Find out what people want by way of a name and call them that.

I note that the Bible seems to be a book of first names—Abraham, Abraham!—Samuel, Samuel!—Martha, Martha!—Simon, Simon!—Saul, Saul!

God wants to be on familiar terms with us. He longs to bring us out of our distresses. The motivation of His heart is only and always love, responsible caring. If we want to live out the life and compassion of Jesus Christ, our reasons have to be his reasons. There is a difference between a Christian care-person and a secular volunteer. It lies within the realm of relationship and motivation. We Christians love because God first loved us. We have Good News to share:

- There is forgiveness—a Savior has come.
- There is hope—we can be made new again.
- There is light at the end of the tunnel of death.

We can pray with and for those we serve. Our practical service may not be any better than that of non-Christians. I have worked with athiests and Muslims and Jewish people who served every bit as selflessly as Christians. It is the Good News that we bring with our service that makes our serving different. Only Christians can tell of a Savior. He is our reason why. But along with that Good News it is essential that like Christ we deal very practically with the felt needs of those who are hurting. He never handed out tracts to the hungry or the sick and went piously on His way. He fed and healed and cared for the whole person.

One of the key factors that led to the success of the Reformation was the emphasis placed on the role of the lay Christian. Luther spoke of the priesthood of all believers. He gave a new meaning to the word vocation, a term that up until then had been applied only to people whose life's work was for the church and in the church. A priest or a monk or a nun had a vocation. But Luther maintained that we all have a vocation before God. We are to do his work wherever he places us. Calvin spoke of the whole world as a monastery. No longer were Christians to cloister themselves behind thick, protective walls of stone. We are to be out in the world serving. The journal of John Wesley is an awe inspiring account of practical service combined with prayer and preaching.

This is our religious heritage. We have a calling, a personal responsibility before God, a ministry that is uniquely our own. Churches are filled with gifted people. The skills that they already possess, that they use unconsciously every day, wait only to be confirmed and reaffirmed. We don't have to be professionals to be of service to others. It is anxiety and uncertainty that holds us back. We want to reach out, but we have all kinds of qualms because we lack confidence—fear of rejection, fear of failure, fear of criticism from others in the church.

When we realize that the stranger we are afraid to approach is a carbon copy of ourselves, it becomes easier. Our needs are the same: clothing, food, shelter, money—material needs. Without these life is threatened. Even when we have these essentials our existence can become intolerable unless we have a sense of belonging. It takes family, friends, community, acceptance, and a feeling of self-worth to satisfy us socially and psychologically. Given all these, our restless hearts still are empty without a sense of God's presence and forgiveness. Faith, hope, love—spiritual needs satisfied fully only by Christ.

When a person faces a crisis, watch for each of these needs. Suppose a man comes to you and asks to borrow five dollars. You can meet that material need by lending him the money. It can stop there. But suppose you notice that he seems anxious and you engage him in kindly conversation. You find out that he needs the money because he has lost his job. As you express your concern for him, he confides that he lost the job because he has a drinking problem. His boss and his co-workers, who gave him many chances have finally given up on him. He has lost their trust and friendship and acceptance.

When you inquire about his family, you learn that because of his drinking his wife and children have left him. He no longer has their love or the sense of belonging he needs so desperately now that he is down and almost out. Social and psychological as well as material needs are not being met.

Even greater is his spiritual need. If you probe his attitudes and understanding, you find that he blames God for his troubles. God could have prevented his boss from firing him. He could have influenced his wife to stand by him. He could have kept him from drinking in the first place. It's all God's fault.

The only need that the man presented, like the tip of an iceberg, was a material one—a request for five dollars. Yet below the surface of that request was an enormous mass of other more desperate needs. We want to be aware of the whole person, not just the need that is apparent. It isn't necessary to know all that is going on in someone's life to be of assistance. Yet it is important to realize that in any hurting situation there is more than meets the eye. Often that which is concealed has a profound influence on how a person in crisis will respond to our overtures of friendship or help.

We all have our various defense mechanisms. I find that Christians can be great pretenders. We feel that it dishonors the Lord to admit to difficulties. Our house has burned down, our child was hit by a truck, our money is gone, but, praise the Lord, everything is all right! Haven't you met that kind of saint? He or she needs to study the Psalms to get a picture of emotional honesty. The psalmists knew how to mourn and cry as well as to sing praises. They were transparently real. So were Jesus and Peter and Paul.

Some of us withdraw when we hurt. We don't pretend. We retreat. We don't want others to know how we hurt. We are afraid that if we let people close to our hearts, we'll break down and cry, that we'll lose control. We keep pain bottled up inside ourselves until an ulcer or asthma or a heart attack forces us to seek healing.

Many times people who are hurting will strike out verbally if we come too close, especially if they haven't requested our help.

All of these defenses are attempts to protect the threatened ego. If we understand this we won't take personally the rejection or anger that we may encounter as we reach out to people in trouble. We will learn to recognize these mechanisms, to sense that they are a type of SOS being signaled unintentionally by the one who is pretending or retreating or attacking. As we gain skill we will learn to respect the pitiful defenses people use to maintain their precarious balance. We learn to wait, to be there, but to wait till God opens the closed door of a human heart. We don't force our way in. Like our Lord, we stand at the door and wait, ready to enter when finally it opens.

It is essential that we be aware or our own limitations. We all have them and we must be honest about them. We won't be able to be of assistance to everyone we find in distress. It's okay to admit that. We can say no when the situation calls for it, but we learn to follow it up by becoming a connecting link to someone who can say yes. It's okay to make a mistake, to say I goofed! That's how we grow. If we're part of a loving, serving fellowship of Christians, we can share our failures as well as our successes and learn from them.

While we are learning new skills, we can draw on old skills that we already possess to take us a long way toward ministering to people in need. We can *listen* well. All the world loves a good listener, one who is attentive, who doesn't interrupt, who will look straight at us with compassion and concern. We can refrain from judging people harshly. We can understand that our standards, our code of conduct, may be foreign to someone who doesn't have our background or upbringing, who never went to the Baptist Sunday school or the Methodist youth group. We learn the difference between a value judgment and a judgment of fact. We keep inviolate the confidence of another, never divulging the personal matters that are shared

with us unless we have permission from that person to
tell a pastor or a doctor or another professional who
will be able to give assistance that we cannot give.

Finally, we can allow people to make their own
decisions. We may explore options, alternatives,
consequences—ask the right questions—but in the
end the course of action to be taken rests with the
person who has the problem, not with us. We set them
free to decide to do nothing, if that is what they wish.
Jesus let people make their own decisions, as he did
with the rich young ruler. He does the same for you
and me every day. He lets us choose which way we
will proceed—or not proceed—again and again.
Sometimes our choices are poor ones. But that
doesn't mean he turns His back on us. Oh no! He lets
us come back to him, to choose again, to try again,
repeatedly. We can be like him in our relationships
with those who may not take our well-meaning
counsel or suggestions. We can set them free to try
other options. And we continue to welcome them as
Christ welcomes us, if they come back to try again. We
never give up on anybody.

. . . — — — . . .

Eleven

The Ministry of Listening

So much has been written about the art of listening, so many workshops given, that most of us groan inwardly when the topic is brought up. "Oh, that again," we sigh. Yet few of us listen well despite the instruction and information we have received. We want to tell *our* story, not listen to someone else's. Whenever a friend or a neighbor or even a stranger starts to relate his or her distress we jump in with, "Let me tell you *my* experience!" Then we pour out our own personal drama, kidding ourselves that we are helping the other person. Instead of helping, we hinder. We load someone who already has trouble with more trouble—our trouble.

Active, conscious listening involves being an attentive audience. When we give people a chance to express themselves, they often come to a clearer comprehension of their situation without any input from us. They reach their own conclusions, form their own plan of action. Just our being there, listening, has enabled them to sort out the tangled web of their predicament.

In my work in the health fields I have had to take many histories. Here are a few tips on listening that have helped me:

Listen to two voices at the same time—that of the distressed person and also the voice of the Holy Spirit within you. God's still, small voice will give you a wisdom far beyond your own natural supply.

Listen for a recurring word or theme, like a discordant note or minor chord in a symphony. The most startling example of this that I can recall involved a young woman on the edge of an emotional breakdown. I was sent to her home to take as complete a life history as I could get, a task that involved several hours. As I painstakingly recorded her story, it occurred to me that she made frequent mention of her older brother, not in a derogatory way, just repeatedly. This man was well known in the community, a successful businessman and government worker, a happily married man with a family.

Suddenly a thought came to me—or that Inner Voice I have learned to trust suggested something to me. It was a long shot and a risky one. I said gently, "You refer often to your brother. Was he ever too intimate with you when you were children?" It was like opening a floodgate. From the time she was six years old her brother had molested her sexually, but she had never before revealed it to anyone. She gave me permission to discuss it with her doctor. Armed with this information, he was able to work with her successfully to bring her back from the brink of mental illness.

Listen to body language as well as to the spoken word.

Often the tongue will be saying yes while the body is screaming no! Tightened jaw muscles, eyelids lowered to conceal eye expression, averted gaze, compressed lips, clenched hands, and a sudden increase of movement of legs or arms all signal that something is amiss. I can tell by watching an audience who in a group is with me or against me. Once when I was speaking to a women's association, I noticed a lady literally turn herself sideways in her chair, trying to turn her back on me. She smoked furiously as I talked, one cigarette after another. She was *not* in favor of what I was proposing!

Listen to the things people don't say.

Some things are glaringly apparent by their absence from the conversation. For example, if a married woman never mentions her husband or her children, one should wonder why.

Listen to parting words.

How many times I have watched someone get up, walk to the door, then, with hand on the knob, look back and say, "Oh, by the way. . . ," or "I forgot to mention. . . ," and then give voice to the real worry and concern.

Up to this point we have been talking about listening skills. The other side of the coin is *enabling,* enabling troubled people to share their distress. There are techniques we can learn to help us to do this, but a word of caution is necessary here. God has given each of us individual personalities. We relate to people differently. Develop your own style and skill through practice and prayer. I have found the following "enablers" effective:

The Direct Approach

Most experts advise caution in the use of direct questions. I find that God has enabled me to use them quite naturally without giving offense. Much depends on timing and tone of voice. When we really care, our concern communicates itself to persons in crisis. Almost always they respond without resentment.

Non-directive Listening

Some people are very gifted with this technique. They say next to nothing other than, "Oh?" "Is that so?" "I think I understand." "How difficult for you!" By encouraging the troubled person to talk it out, healing comes.

Confrontation

A psychiatrist taught me the value of this technique, especially when dealing with alcoholics or others who evade and deny. "Jack" (or Jill), "you are drinking too much. Your family knows it, your friends know it, and your boss knows it. You need to know it. I want you to keep track of every drink you take in the next twenty-four hours. Write it down and keep count so that you have an accurate picture of what you are consuming."

Sometimes this will turn the tide in a drinking pattern. It did for a close friend of mine.

The Universal

I was taught to use this technique in the nurse-midwifery clinic, where it was important to find out if a pregnancy was planned, and whether the couple wanted the baby. We could honestly say, "Probably over 50 percent of the women who come to our clinic are dismayed when they learn for certain that they are pregnant. They just aren't ready for a new arrival!

They worry about the expense involved and how their husbands will take the news. How is it with you and Jack? Will a baby fit into your lives comfortably just now?"

That gave the woman the chance to identify with over half of the female population coming to the clinic, to say, "Oh, no! We can't afford to have a baby at this time. Jack will be very upset!" It gave us the chance to counsel competently.

Anticipatory Guidance

In this technique *we* say the words that the person cannot say. We anticipate the real problem that he or she cannot verbalize. We speak about the dreaded thing ourselves. Here is another example from the nurse-midwifery clinic.

A young Spanish-speaking woman came to us late in pregnancy for prenatal care. When the doctor examined her, he realized that the sexual aspect of her marriage had to be very difficult and painful for her. The opening of the vaginal canal was still almost totally closed. She had made no mention of difficulty during the initial interview. Taking her cue from the doctor, a bilingual nurse-midwife casually and matter of factly commented to the patient that after the birth of the baby sexual relations with her husband would no longer be difficult. The woman burst into tears of relief. She confided that her husband was talking of divorce.

Both in your listening and in your enabling, be casual, unshockable, and have a good memory. Almost always, if we think back, we can recall something in our past that will help us to identify with a present problem.

One morning an elementary school principal asked me to "deal" with a child who had brought a pornographic magazine into the classroom. She was no more than eight or nine years old. As I walked down the hall toward the classroom I thought, "Well Lord, what do I do with this?" Instantly I was transported back in time. There I was in the back yard with my playmates. We were curious. A group of our brothers, off in a corner, were laughing over a grubby magazine one of them held. After a while they threw it down and went off to play baseball. We girls picked up the magazine. It was filled with pictures of nude women in suggestive poses. As I remember, it meant little to us. We looked through it, cast it aside, went back to our play. No adult was around to make a federal case out of it.

All this was going through my mind as I led the weeping youngster into the school yard where we could talk privately. She had taken the magazine from a trash can where some boys had put it. History repeating itself. I explained that I understood her curiosity and shared my own experience with her. We agreed to discard the magazine in a place where it wouldn't cause any more difficulty.

During that day at least five faculty members sidled up to me with smirks to ask what I had done with "that" magazine. One of them was an ordained minister working as a substitute teacher. I suspect that they needed counseling more than the child did.

Pornography is a vicious evil that we need to attack with all our might. But there is no need to lay 'heavies' on little children who innocently stumble on to it. To be a good listener means not letting your emotional reaction against an evil be wrongly directed toward innocent people.

A chapter on communication isn't complete without a reference to the art of interviewing—getting the facts. At times listening alone isn't enough.

Enabling a person to talk isn't enough. We must obtain the information—the facts—that are necessary for setting up a plan of action.

If you have to be an advocate someday for a person who is in need of assistance from a secular or governmental agency, you will find out very quickly how essential it is to have all the facts at your fingertips. Although it is important to be aware of emotions and feelings, both our own and those of the person in crisis, we must not let them cloud the issues involved.

Get the facts first—complete name, address, phone number, age, birthdate, marital status, number of children, place of employment, etc. Know what the actual needs are. Does the person need food or shelter or legal advice or money for rent or a job? We want to be able to assist this person in distress to see the situation clearly, to understand the options available, and to weigh the alternatives and the consequences of each possibility. In short, our goal is to know how to assist someone to set up a plan of action.

. . . _ _ _ . . .

Twelve

Setting Up a Plan of Action

It has been estimated that 25 billion dollars of federal allotments to tax-exempt agencies—organizations that have been providing human services—will be cut, over a five-year period. With God's help and a strategy of service, we can develop a philosophy in our churches that says, "THE BUCK STOPS HERE." What can *we* do ourselves to help those in distress in our community?

In a situation where there is a pressing need for immediate temporary assistance not readily available through official sources, a church with an SOS ministry can call out its reserves without delay. Provisions for emergency relief—food, clothes, shelter, child care, enough money to sustain life—can be tapped almost at once. That is why plans for giving such service must be developed ahead of time, not at the moment of crisis. We then can fill the gap until other sources of assistance are worked out. The majority of human needs are for temporary material or physical help, needs that can be met by any Christian congregation with a strategy of service.

Yet there will be times when it will be necessary to refer someone to an outside source of assistance, times when we cannot alleviate a need situation ourselves. It is then that we act as advocates. We stand by the person until the service is secured. Our perfect example, of course, is Jesus Christ the Righteous One, who is our Advocate with the Father. He has promised that he will never leave us alone, that he will speak and work on our behalf.

That is what we are to do as advocates for people in trouble. Our role is to assist the person in crisis to look at options, alternatives, and possible consequences so that the choice of a plan of action will be an informed one, as constructive and responsible as possible. Once we determine the facts of the case and the actual needs, we go over the personal community resources available. Are there family members, neighbors, friends, a church fellowship that can be called upon? Or is it necessary to appeal to social service agencies?

The final decision regarding a plan of action must be made by the person in need. This includes deciding to do nothing, to refuse to act at all. Only in life-threatening situations would we take matters into our own hands. Keeping a confidence or respecting an individual's wishes is not as binding as saving a life. Under ordinary circumstances we avoid taking over. We encourage the one who is in trouble to make as many arrangements as he or she is capable of planning. It is wise to jot down who will do what before getting together again, a reminder for everyone involved.

Above all, Christians should apply the balm of prayer. Let it be known that you are a person of prayer, that God's great help is available. Rarely is prayer refused by anyone in crisis. Most often it is accepted with pathetic eagerness. Religious differences fade into oblivion. In a hospital where I once worked an elderly Catholic nun visited and prayed with each patient at bedtime. Whether Catholic, Protestant, or Jewish, everyone welcomed her faithful intercession.

If a situation is such that a person must be referred to a social service agency, underscore the following fact in your thinking: *A referral is not complete until the service is obtained.* It is not enough to make a phone call to an agency to tell them about someone's trouble or to write out a note of referral for the person to take to an agency. The people who need our help often are frightened, bewildered, sick, frail, or elderly. They may not be able to cope with long lines or the confusion of the average agency. They can get lost in the shuffle in no time. If they feel faint or exhausted or need to sit down, they just drop out. If they need to go to a restroom, they may lose their place in line.

A few years ago an effort was made in Boston to find advocates to accompany the frail elderly who went to the out-patient department of one of the city's famous hospitals. Too often they failed to make it into the system. It was all too complicated, too exhausting. If our parents or grandparents were the ones trying to find help, we wouldn't dream of letting them go alone to a crowded clinic or a government agency.

For an eyeopener drop in at the local welfare office some day to watch what goes on. Or better yet, try calling on the phone. Chances are you will get the busy signal for an hour or two before someone answers. Then you will be put on hold for another half hour. And so on. Or look at the forms that must be completed by those asking for aid. Imagine trying to fill them out if your eyesight is poor or your hand shakes or you don't understand English. We must make every effort to go with those who must be referred to a government or secular agency, to stick like Jacob wrestling with the angel till we actually know that the need is being met. If necessary, we can set up a relay of advocates to relieve one another at two hour intervals rather than tying up one SOS Christian for a longer period of time in a clinic waiting room.

Advocacy calls for assertiveness. But there is a difference between worldly assertiveness and that of Jesus Christ. Christian assertiveness is appropriate, not rude. It is persistent but polite. Name calling, threats, or abusiveness do not bring honor to our Lord. We should be courteous toward the official with whom we are dealing but should not back down. We have a right to request and receive correct information, to be given the guidelines that determine a person's eligibility for service.

If we get the run-around, we should not hesitate to insist, politely but firmly, to speak to a supervisor and to go on up the bureaucratic ladder until we get satisfactory explanations. If the one for whom we are an advocate is said to be ineligible for assistance from a tax-supported agency, we should challenge that decision. Well over half of those decisions, if appealed, are reversed. If the decision is upheld, we need to look to other resources.

Nearly every community has some type of resource directory in print. Every church should purchase one. It is impossible to keep up with all the sources of help that exist, especially in a large city. The picture is too massive, too complex for anyone to know it all. Add to that the fact that changes in agency policies and benefits are occurring almost daily because of financial cutbacks. But we can be familiar with a few key agencies, a few key resource people, and their phone numbers so that we may obtain up-to-date information when a need arises. Most cities now have an information and referral center that can be called for advice. Every church should have that number on file. If there is no information and referral service, usually the local health department or the social service division of a community hospital can suggest an appropriate referral.

Never feel satisfied because an agency assigns a case worker or social worker to follow up on a person you are befriending. Realize that that worker may have scores of other "clients to process." Hang in there and let it be known that you are hanging in there until the need is actually met. Remember, the need for friendship never ceases. It may be through you that this person will come to a realization of what a Friend we have in Jesus.

The crucial step to be taken by each one of us is that of personal commitment. It is time for us to put ourselves on the line. No one who belongs to Christ can side-step his call to servanthood. Just before Jesus fed the five thousand, his disciples came to him and said, "Send the crowds away, so they can go to the villages and buy themselves some food" (Matt. 14:15).

Obviously the Twelve were tired and over-whelmed by the needs of the multitude. But what did Jesus say? "They do not need to go away. You give them something to eat!" (v. 16). The disciples protested, "We have here only five loaves of bread and two fish" (v. 17). Yet given to Christ their little became more than enough.

Perhaps some of you are saying, "I don't have any skills or gifts. There's nothing I can do." Yes there is. *Everyone,* young or old, can do something the

Lord can use. Everyone has some "loaves and fishes." If you can write a card or dial a phone or bake a casserole dish or fill out a form or drive a car or pound a nail, it can be put to God's use and glory.

I have a friend in Chicago who said, "Willie, I can't do anything except drive." "All right, Lou," I answered, I'll put you down for driving only." Do you know, there were more calls for Lou's transportation than for any other service. I could have given him an assignment every day.

Being retired or being a senior citizen doesn't let you off the hook either. My mother, at the age of eighty-six, still lived alone in her tiny house in New England. Although she was becoming increasingly frail, she continued to be very much interested in her garden, her grandchildren, and in the events of the world around her. One day my brother, who was connected with the city government, explained to her that efforts were being made by a certain night club in town to include nude dancers in the floor show. This may be old hat in some places but not where my mother lived. He said that at the city council meeting where this matter was reviewed, only one person appeared to express opposition—a Roman Catholic priest whose church was near the night club in question.

This weighed on my mother's mind. She was a quiet, little homebody, not given to protests of demonstrations, but she was a commited Christian. Before the next city council meeting, when the issue would come up again, she turned to the yellow pages in the phone book to where churches are listed. She called them all, informing them of what was under consideration and suggesting that they send representatives to the meeting. She did all this without discussing it with any of the family and without identifying herself on the phone—which perhaps was fortunate for my brother's career. At that next crucial city council meeting the room was crowded with Christians. One man actually stood up and preached a sermon. Without further discussion the council turned down the night club's request.

That wasn't the end of it. The battle has gone on. Yet one small, aged woman, with a telephone in her hand and Christ in her heart, was able to turn back principalities and powers. We could have an army of people like that in our churches if we would start challenging our elderly Christians out of the Word of God to undertake tasks of service. I have every confidence that if the senior members of our churches were enlisted and briefed on how to wage an attack on pornography and objectionable TV programming, these things would change. It takes numbers, votes, time, and above all, commitment. Backed by prayer and linked with God's power, they could accomplish wonders. It doesn't have to be sunrise-sunset for any of us when we belong to the Lord Jesus. It can be sunset-sunrise just as long as we let Him live His life through us.

· · ·   — — —   · · ·

Thirteen

Clues for Continuing

After commitment, what next? Making a decision to serve is one thing. Turning a commitment into action is another. It is at this point that most good beginnings fail. What contributes to success? Let me offer some guidelines.

> *Specify your geographic boundaries and service limits.*

To avoid any misunderstanding about what we are attempting, our expectations must be clearly defined, our focus spelled out. We are talking about a volunteer fire department approach to meeting individual human needs in the local community around our church. Before we do anything else, we must establish our geographic boundaries and service limits. We are not proposing a twenty-four-hour emergency service to cover the entire city or county.

Through networking and referral, we can participate in an expanded ministry, but our first responsibility lies within the community where our church stands.

This does not preclude contributing resources and expertise to neighborhoods where the needs are greater than in our own. Grim experience indicates, however, that those living in poverty areas resent it when Lady Bountiful from affluent society attempts to give a few volunteer hours in areas of squalor. It is wiser to equip those who reside there, to provide training, supplies, and backup to poorer churches that want to have an SOS ministry of their own. Affluent neighborhoods are not without those who need our service ministries. Loneliness, divorce, alcoholism, drug abuse, suicide, bankruptcy, disability, and illness may be kept in the closet, but they are there.

For a simple way to map out an area of action, draw a large circle on a blackboard. At the top of the circle write North; at the bottom, South; then East and West at the sides.

Draw lines through the circle to divide it into four equal quadrants. Color code these four sections with a crayon mark. Northeast can be blue, Northwest can be green, southeast yellow, and southwest pink. Put a cross in the center of the circle. That is your church.

What are your natural boundaries? Perhaps your denomination has a parish system (Lutheran, Episcopalian, Catholic). If so, your boundaries are those of the parish. Write in the streets or river or railroad that mark your north, south, east, and west borders.

If your denomination doesn't have the parish system, you must establish your own boundaries of service. Consult a detailed map when you do this.

Next, put a tiny cross for every other church that falls within the circle. Put the name of each church in small letters under each cross. You may want to add some other symbol to your circle to indicate hospitals or nursing homes or health facilities if there are any within your boundaries.

How to Define an Area of Action
Sample Map

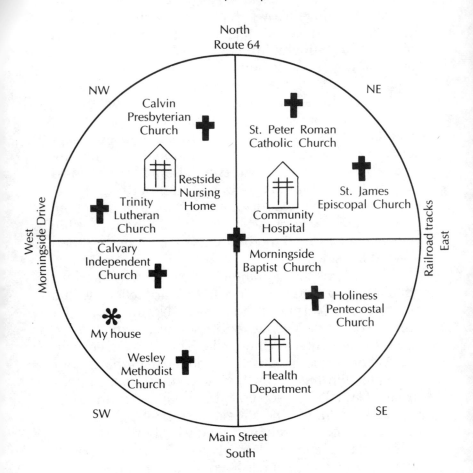

Finally, put a star where you live within the circle. Or, if you commute to your church from beyond the circle, put your star beside the quadrant closest to your home. Print your name under the star. When we find people in need, we try to link them to SOS Christians who live nearest to them. Although it isn't always possible to do this, and one may be asked to serve anywhere within the circle, it conserves time and fuel to keep the distances involved short. When we set up our SOS card file we color code it so that we know at a glance which volunteers living in a certain section of our circle are willing to do a specific task.

What type of services are we prepared to give? The commitment form in appendix 1 lists twelve suggestions. It is only a sample. Needs differ from community to community and from church to church. You will want to do a preliminary assessment of the needs of the area where your church stands before designing your commitment form, so that it reflects the services you are prepared to give. It is pointless to offer assistance that is not in demand.

I am not suggesting that you develop an in-depth, dragged-out community survey that will remain forever on the drawing board! Serving, like witnessing, must begin at once. The longer we put if off, the more excuses we can find for not starting at all. Begin with the situations you know about within the congregational family, then branch out to those living around the church.

Keep reaching out.

The most basic method of outreach, of active, continuing case-finding, is for each one of us to be watching for individuals who may require our assistance. Those in need may not seek us, especially if they are elderly. We have to be on the lookout for them. Never assume that needs are being met by family or friends. If you hear or suspect that someone is in distress, visit the person. Check out the situation yourself.

Other ways to find people in need:

- Mail a pastoral letter to all those within the church family who are elderly or infirm or home-bound, telling them of the SOS ministry. This often brings requests for help. One minister mentioned in his letter that soon two SOS Christians would be coming to visit. Long before the assessment calls were completed, lonely shut-ins were asking, "When will I be visited? When will they get to me?"
- Appeal to other churches within the circle to learn of needs through them. Tell them what you are doing. Invite them to help, to share in this ministry of outreach. Suggest clustering. If enough churches would cluster, we soon could have a series of intersecting circles giving total coverage to a city or town or countryside.
- Approach those who are human-service providers in the community—doctors, public health and visiting nurses, social workers, home care personnel, information and referral staff, hospital workers. Ask for referrals to those who need practical love and concern.
- Contact other service providers. The police, mail deliverers, pharmacists, beauticians, laundromat attendants, and bartenders often are the first to know about the sorrows of the community.
- Offer a much needed service: transportation, chore service, help with personal care, assistance with filling out forms for those whose eyesight or handwriting or knowledge of En-

glish is inadequate. Let it be known that you
are willing to give this kind of assistance, and
you will have an immediate response.

- Do a door-to-door canvas of the community
around your church, visiting every home.
Distribute a letter of introduction a day or two
before starting to canvas. Slip the letters under
doors or put them in hallways. Do not place
them in mailboxes, as it is a violation of postal
regulations. It is wise to notify the police before
canvassing. If you work out from the center of
the area to be canvassed, you will utilize the
natural channel of the "grapevine." Word-of-
mouth advertising travels rapidly outward,
making a more receptive public as the canvas
progresses. Although some people may be
unwilling to talk to you, those who do can be
counted on to spread the word that you are not
after money or pledges. Have good iden-
tification—if possible, an ID card with a photo-
graph that links you with the church or
churches involved. Employ the gospel pattern
of outreach. Christ first sent the Twelve then
the Seventy out two by two. No one went
alone. The buddy system does much to overcome anxiety. Go out two by two, preferably a
man and a woman together. Canvas during the
daylight hours. My own experience with canvassing underscored the need for patience,
persistence, and endurance. Expect and prepare for bad weather! I knocked on many
doors and rang many bells the first day out, but
found few people who would even talk to me
in the hall or on the porch. On day two, the
reception was much less guarded. By day
three, everyone seemed to know about me,

especially the lonely and the troubled. Students enrolled in a seminary course I taught did a door-to-door canvas in the neighborhood around the school. To their surprise, the assistance most frequently requested was for help to learn English, a service they were well able to provide. Many families of Spanish or Korean background had moved into the area. It is only by getting out into the homes around our churches that we can discover, through listening, the felt needs of the people near by. As we meet their felt needs they may discover, just as we did at one pivotal point in our lives, that the greatest need of all is to experience the love and redemption of God through Jesus Christ.

Have an ongoing recruitment effort.

Try to offer a wide variety of volunteer activity so that the talents of many can be utilized—tasks that interest men and young people as well as activities for women and seniors and retirees. Respect choices. Do not assign tasks or times that have not been agreed upon. Recruiting on a one-to-one basis is time consuming, but it is the most effective means of securing volunteers. Ask new recruits to recommend others who might be willing to volunteer. Keep the congregation aware of your ministries. Encourage SOS volunteers to speak at church functions. Take advantage of opportunities to talk about the service, to give human interest accounts, and to invite others to take part. Recognition and praise from the pulpit creates interest. Be ready for the moment when interest and enthusiasm peak. Give people the opportunity to respond with action, to commit themselves to specific service ministries. Have pledge forms readily available. Everyone, even the busiest person, can schedule in one service a month. Housewives, students, teenagers, professionals, loners—especially loners—people of all races and nationalities and languages form a great potential source of assistance.

Secure a support system.

It is crucial to have resource people to turn to for backup and information when it is needed. The pastor's spiritual and practical counsel means more to SOS Christians than most clergy realize. Unless laity feel that the pastor shares in their ministry, they soon become discouraged. In addition to the pastor, nearly every congregation has within its membership professionals who are willing to advise, to share their expertise. If not, make arrangements with someone outside the church to give this kind of guidance. Often denominational headquarters will have a social service person on staff.

Perhaps the most essential ingredient for success is the support that volunteers give to one another. Frequent contact for the purpose of sharing and prayer as well as to accept assignments and to give reports seems to be the lifeblood of an SOS ministry. We all need encouragement. Our morale needs sustaining. Expressions of appreciation and recognition help us to keep on keeping on. Without them, even the most enthusiastic volunteer soon grows discouraged. If we expect thanks from those we serve, we may be deeply disappointed. Even our Lord was not immune to ingratitude. When he cleansed ten lepers and only one returned to express thanks, he said to his disciples—sorrowfully, I imagine—"Were not all ten cleansed? Where are the other nine?"

(Luke 17:17). The ingratitude of humanity can over-whelm and embitter us unless our brothers and sisters in Christ uphold us.

There are so many ways to show appreciation. A pat on the back, on-the-job praise, or a little note of thanks often means more than formal awards. A yearly commissioning service adds deep meaning to the SOS commitment we make before God. But it is the regular monthly get-togethers that maintain a sense of accountability, that make us aware of what others are doing, that give us a chance to express appreciation to someone who may need to be encouraged.

Exchange leadership functions at the monthly meetings frequently. If two people have been respon-sible for the SOS file box for three months, relieve them. Give two others the opportunity to preside. Where does the SOS box stay between meetings? In the church where the pastor and his secretary have access to it. It should not be taken to anyone's home. Needs will arise between monthly meetings. Those in the church office must be able to reach an SOS contact person who will secure a volunteer. Many needs are not of an emergency nature and can wait for review at the monthly meeting. But food, clothing, shelter, and transportation to medical help are needs that cannot wait.

Avoid the pitfall of the "takeover." If one person tries to do everything, whether the minister or a layperson, it will prove detrimental to all the others who want to serve, who want to grow to maturity in Christ. I have seen this tragic happening in more than one church. Soon the general response is, "Let Joe do it," or "Ask Mary. That's her baby!" When Joe or Mary collapse, so does the service.

Pray without ceasing.

Pray for one another and for those whom you befriend. Pray in season and out of season to be Christ's people in the community where your church stands. Have a deep commitment to Christ and to his church. If we belong to him and to one another, we have a solid foundation on which to build a structure for our strategy of service.

. . . — — — . . .

Fourteen

Another Possibility

Unexpected circumstances took me back to Hawaii shortly after I completed my seminary studies. During the few months that I was there I tried a different approach. Instead of going to individual churches, I went to denominational headquarters to talk about an SOS ministry. I explored the possibility of a training program that could be extended to all the churches within a given denomination.

The Southern Baptists gave the most attentive ear to my proposal. I attribute this mainly to the sensitivity of the acting director of the Women's Missionary Union, a keen, capable, beautiful woman who knew at once what I was talking about. Women in general catch on to the concept of local servanthood more readily than men. Having fulfilled a servant's role for centuries, perhaps women are more aware of the basic needs of their neighbors.

One other circumstance influenced the Baptists. My mother had spent a winter with me in Hawaii before I entered seminary. Of course, she faithfully attended a Baptist church. The minister, remembering her, gave me a vote of confidence! Once again Providence opened a door to me because of my mother. Never underestimate the influence of quiet Christians who pray much and say little.

If you haven't visited Hawaii recently, perhaps you think that the Aloha spirit is such that there is little need for SOS ministry in that Pacific paradise. Regrettably, Hawaii, like every other state, is changing. The pressures that affect people in New York City and Chicago and Los Angeles affect people in Honolulu. From 1960 to 1980 Oahu's population leaped from a little over 294,000 to nearly 763,000. In the last decade crime skyrocketed 147 percent in Hawaii. In 1980, on Oahu alone, there were 595 confirmed cases of child abuse. Hawaii is in the throes of transition, with symptoms of family breakdown increasingly apparent. It doesn't seem to matter where one goes in our American society; there are evidences of the same decay eating away at the foundations that have held so long. I have worked in rural and isolated villages, in middle income and wealthy suburbia, and in metropolitan cities, with their slums and affluence trying to co-exist. The picture everywhere is the same. I do not know of any community that does not need an SOS ministry.

I learned in Hawaii that denominational wheels turn very slowly. One must not arrive in the autumn with a bright idea and expect it to be implemented rapidly. It took until December simply to schedule an opportunity for me to speak to the Baptist clergy at their monthly meeting. They were an attentive, thoughtful audience. Many came to see me afterwards to express interest, some to request workshops immediately. At that point I began to discover the frustrations of trying to schedule workshops into already

tightly filled church calendars. There are over forty
Baptist churches in the Hawaiian Islands. Between
January and April I succeeded in reaching only three
of them. Before I could do more it was necessary for
me to return to the east coast. My mother was dying.

The director of the Women's Missionary Union
promptly announced that she would conduct the
workshop scheduled for May, since it was to be held in
the church she attended. I gave her the materials I had
prepared, feeling confident that she could follow the
simple format and add to it out of her own rich
experience and wisdom. She was able to do this and
succeeded in setting up an SOS ministry in her own
church. It is my prayer that she will go on to the other
Southern Baptist churches on the Islands until all have
an SOS ministry. They are capable of networking the
entire Hawaiian chain and of providing a model for
every other denomination.

This approach is one that needs further explora-
tion. The structures of Protestantism are such that
funding for educational and/or mission-outreach efforts are almost always tied into denominational
offices—state, regional, national. I can envision every
church across our country with an SOS ministry. Why
not? Every church has a Sunday school. Every church
has a young people's program. These started long ago
when the need for them was recognized by a few
caring people. The concepts caught on and were
incorporated into the ministry of all churches everywhere. If training materials and resource people were
made available through denominational headquarters,
local churches could develop their own SOS ministries
under the guidance and direction of their own gifted
laity. It is an idea whose time has come.

Recently the pastor of a large city church assert-
ed, "You'll never get Baptists or Evangelicals to do

this! They have no social conscience, most of them. Oh, perhaps here and there you will find the exceptional church that cares about the poor and the oppressed locally, but it is a rare exception. You're looking to the wrong people; you're in the wrong circles."

It interested me that the pastor went on to remark, rather pensively, I thought, "Of course, it takes only a year or two of this kind of involvement to wear one down to nothing. It is impossible to keep on with only good intentions to sustain us. There has to be something more—something solid for a foundation."

There has to be something more, *something solid.*

> The church's one foundation
> is Jesus Christ her Lord.
>
> On Christ the Solid Rock we stand,
> All other ground is sinking sand,
> All other ground is sinking sand.

For this unrelenting warfare we must be strong in the Lord and in the strength of His might:

> "Finally, be strong in the Lord and in his mighty power. Put on the full armor of God so that you can take your stand against the devil's schemes. For our struggle is not against flesh and blood, but against the rulers, against the authorities, against the powers of this dark world and against the spiritual forces of evil in the heavenly realms. Therefore put on the full armor of God, so that when the day of evil comes, you may be able to stand your ground, and after you have done everything, to stand. Stand firm then, with the belt of truth buckled around your waist, with the breastplate of righteousness in place, and

with your feet fitted with the gospel of peace. In addition to all this, take up the shield of faith, with which you can extinguish all the flaming arrows of the evil one. Take the helmet of salvation and the sword of the Spirit, which is the word of God. And pray in the Spirit on all occasions with all kinds of prayers and requests. With this in mind be on the alert and always keep on praying for all the saints." (Eph 6:10–18).

This is God's bedrock for our strategy of service.

· · · — — — · · ·

POSTSCRIPT:
ONCE AGAIN, LIGHTLY

A plea for "a complete training process plan, an outline or summary of everything needed for an SOS ministry" is a request I anticipate from some of my readers. Even if this were possible it would be both impractical and undesirable.

Ideally, a strategy of service is tailored to fit the needs of an individual church. The aspirations of a particular congregation, the neighborhood in which the church stands, and the resources within both the community and the church itself all must be taken into consideration. Every SOS ministry will differ to a lesser or greater degree. Some churches have responded enthusiastically to the concept of clustering. Others, from a separatist standpoint, are not in favor of this approach. These preferences are to be respected carefully. It is only out of the framework of each worshiping community that a strategy of service may be drawn.

In SOS I have tried to trace my own journey into service, to highlight both failures and successes in my fumbling attempts to find out what works when a church commits itself to local service ministries and endeavors to carry out that commitment. More specifics are contained in this written account than I would include in the average SOS workshop. I prefer the light touch, the soft sell. SOS is not intended to be a procedure book. It is at best a book of suggestions, of clues, for grass-roots outreach. God forbid that any one formula be adhered to slavishly or that the charisma of an individual be essential for success.

If there is one concept that I have hoped to get across it is this: *Every church has within itself the potential for reaching out effectively to the community in which it stands.* The giftedness of those quiet Christians sitting in the pews never ceases to astound me. *Any* strategy that will tap the collective know-how of a congregation and channel the particular gifts and skills of individual Christians into practical, workable avenues of service is acceptable. *It is imperative to have a strategy of some kind,* a prearranged plan of action that becomes operative swiftly and surely when a need arises. Chapters 8, 9, and 13 are especially helpful in that regard.

For the sake of those who want to hear it again, review may be helpful. A strategy of service involves the following:

Commitment to Christ and to one another

Without a living relationship to Christ, we cannot carry out his service mandate. Because that mandate often confronts us with a relentless tide of human tragedy and woe, he has set us in a fellowship. We are not alone. We draw strength from him and from one another. As we learn to share the load together, we find that the burden truly is light.

The essential participation of the pastor

Almost certainly an SOS ministry will fail without a supportive pastor. A congregation looks to its minister for a green light, as well as for continuing confirmation. Awareness of need, approval of involvement, appropriate action have their origins in the pulpit. Both the undergirding and the setting free to serve are singular clergy contributions.

Assessment—within and outside the church
What are the needs, resources, goals? We want to set specific geographical boundaries and service limits, to spell out carefully what we hope to accomplish.

Training for service
We discover the universality of need and ways to alleviate need. We learn to recognize our own gifts, to be conscious of communication skills we use unconsciously every day, and to use them more effectively. If specific tasks call for specific training, we make arrangements for that training.

Backup system
We need to feel that we are not alone. If we are uncertain in a helping situation we must know that there is someone we can contact for counsel and direction—the pastor or a community worker or an information and referral center.

Structuring for service
Many hands make light work. Through shared leadership and short-term commitments, we minister to our community. To avoid a takeover by one or two persons, we rotate responsibilities regularly. We consider clustering churches to network our neighborhood.

Accountability
Frequent, scheduled get-togethers to receive assignments and to report on those we have served, keep us on our toes and allow us to evaluate our progress. Worship, praise, instruction, support, appreciation, and consolation are the ingredients of an SOS meeting.

Confidentiality
We learn to be the priest in the confessional as

we share the lives of those we serve. We do not betray a confidence.

Active, ongoing recruitment

Service is the mandate of the Bible for every believer, not just for a chosen few. Invite all church members to take part in the SOS ministry—not only a general invitation, but an individual seeking-out of those who are uninvolved. Fit the task to the person.

Prayer

In season, out of season, alone and together— never stop praying.

Appendix 1

COMMITMENT FORM

(Adapted from a form developed by Catholic Charities Parish Community Services, Chicago.)

To help Jesus Christ be visible in this community, I am willing to volunteer the following services at least once a month:

_____ ASSESSMENT VISITING to determine needs, offer support, plan services

_____ FRIENDLY VISITING to the lonely, sick, shut-in; home ___ hospital ___ phone ___

_____ TRANSPORTATION to doctor, clinic, hospital, church; ___ Help with moving ___

_____ SHOPPING for persons who cannot get out or who have no transportation

_____ LIGHT HOUSEHOLD CHORES: indoor ___ outdoor ___ minor repairs ___

_____ EMERGENCY FOOD: meal preparation ___ meal delivery ___

_____ PERSONAL CARE: sponge bath, washing hair, dressing, etc.

_____ RESPITE SERVICE: provide a few hours relief for those with constant care of dependents

_____ TEMPORARY OVERNIGHT SHELTER for the homeless

_____ TUTORING: of adults and/or children

_____ ADVOCACY: to assist or accompany those requiring help from various social, governmental or legal offices

_____ OTHER (please list any other service or skill that you could provide: _____

_____

Name _____

Address _____ Phone _____

Days available _____

Times available _____

Age _____

Please be realistic about your time. One service a month that is faithfully carried out is better than a weekly assignment that is not completed. Thank you for caring.

S   O   S

. . . _ _ _ . . .

Appendix 2

FILE CARDS

Sections 1 and 2 of the card file contain identical copies of this card, filed first alphabetically by last name and then in the second section by catagory of service, thus providing two ways of keeping track of volunteers.

Section 3 of the card file identifies those in need of services and records the services rendered.

```
Name _____
            Last              First              Initial

Address _____

        _____ Zip _____

Phone _____

Birthdate _____

Days and times available:



Services

```

FRONT

Name _____
        Last   First   Initial

Address _____

_____ Zip _____

Birthdate _____ Age ____ Phone _____

Date of contact _____ How received? _____

Physical condition _____

Spiritual condition _____

Needs to be met:

BACK

DATE	VOLUNTEER	FINDINGS AND FOLLOW-UP NEEDED

Appendix 3

S O S VOLUNTEER SERVICE RECORD

Church _____ Year _____

Name	Jan.	Feb.	Mar.	Apr.	May	June	July	Aug.	Sept.	Oct.	Nov.	Dec.

Appendix 4

Certificate of Achievement

This is to certify that

_____

has completed the specialized course of training in

STRATEGY OF SERVICE

Granted this _____ day of _____, 19____

at _____

_____
Pastor

_____
Instructor

88605